# DARE
## TO
## FORGIVE

# DARE
# TO
# FORGIVE

## Edward M. Hallowell, M.D.

Health Communications, Inc.
Deerfield Beach, Florida

www.hcibooks.com

We gratefully acknowledge permission to reprint the following cited material: Robert Frost, "Forgive, O Lord" and "Dust of Snow" from *The Poetry of Robert Frost*, edited by Edward Connery Lathem. Copyright 1923, ©1969 by Henry Holt and Company, copyright 1951, ©1962 by Robert Frost. Reprinted with the permission of Henry Holt and Company, LLC.

**Library of Congress Cataloging-in-Publication Data**

Hallowell, Edward M.
　　Dare to forgive / Edward M. Hallowell.
　　　　p. cm.
　　Includes bibliographical references.
　　ISBN 0-7573-0010-3 (tp)
　　1. Forgiveness. I. Title.

　　BF637.F67H35 2004
　　155.9'2—dc22

　　　　　　　　　　　　　　　　　　　　　　　　2003068582

A Human Moments® Book
©2004 Edward M. Hallowell, M.D.
ISBN 0-7573-0010-3

Publisher: Health Communications, Inc.
　　　　　　3201 S.W. 15th Street
　　　　　　Deerfield Beach, Florida 33442-8190

*Cover design by Lawna Patterson Oldfield*
*Inside book design by Dawn Von Strolley Grove*

For
Peter Metz

# Contents

# A Note on the Cover

On the cover of this book, a little bluebird sits on a wire, and the same bird appears in other places in the book. I wanted to explain why the bluebird is here.

My mother taught me more about forgiveness than anyone else. She had a very hard life, full of disappointments and pain. However, she never, ever lost her optimism, hope and positive spirit. She never held a grudge. Although she could get angry, she always forgave. One of the maxims she lived by was, "Never go to bed angry."

One of her favorite symbols of happiness was the bluebird. For that reason, I asked the publishers of this book if they could possibly find a bluebird to put on the cover. I love the image they found. Like my mother, and like forgiveness itself, this bird stands alone, vulnerable but brave.

# Acknowledgments

I love the acknowledgments section of books. As a writer, I know how heartfelt the words in these sections usually are. I fear that many readers skip over this section, because, after all, the acknowledgments section is not the reason they bought the book. However, while writers write alone, every book is a group effort. For me, my twelfth-grade English teacher is coauthor of everything I write. For others, it might be an editor, a spouse, a buddy or even a dog. My point is that you can learn a lot about the writer and the book by reading the acknowledgments.

This book appeared out of nowhere. I was standing at the door of an auditorium in which I was about to give a lecture on happiness when a person standing next to me asked what I planned to write my next book about. "I am thinking about writing a book about forgiveness," I said. I had never thought such a thing. I have no idea where that remark came from. However, it wasn't a lie, because the moment I spoke the words, I knew that's what I wanted to do. Therefore, the first person I must thank is that anonymous woman who asked me what I was planning to do next.

Once I started in on forgiveness, just about everybody I spoke to helped me. Some helped me with their stories, like the two cab drivers whose stories you will find in this book, the woman whose son was killed on September 11 and my friend in Seattle who threw a stone at a window for reasons you'll discover early in the book.

Will McDonough, the great Boston sportswriter who died in the winter of 2003, helped me by showing how hidden a forgiving attitude can be. Will had a reputation for being a tough guy, a guy who got even, a guy who didn't forgive. I came to know him only a few months before he died. I wanted to write a book about him but was brought up short when he said, "The trouble with this book is I don't want to hurt anybody, and to make the book interesting I'd have to tell the truth and a lot of people would get hurt." So we nixed the idea of the book and planned a book about the New England Patriots instead. Will died before we could get that off the ground. However, I will always treasure the gift of the all-too-brief friendship we had. Will McDonough was one of the most interesting, most intelligent, most engaging, most honest men I have ever met. We all miss you, Willy.

Charles Bennison, Episcopal bishop in Philadelphia; Tom Shaw, Episcopal bishop in Boston; and Bob Tobin, rector of Christ Church in Cambridge all helped me with their extensive knowledge and capacious hearts. Charles pointed me to Hannah Arendt, whose thinking is central to the main thesis of this book. Tom helped me by shaping some of my ideas when they were still on the pottery wheel. Bob inspired me with weekly sermons that always stressed the importance of finding a nonviolent way to peace.

However, this book is not primarily a political book. It is a personal book aimed at people's personal lives. I would like to write down the name of every friend I have who has ever forgiven me; it would be a very long list! I thank them all for helping me to learn about forgiveness personally.

Of course, I thank my agent, Jill Kneerim, for her extraordinary care and attention to my needs and foibles. She is the best!

I also am grateful to Tom Sand, Bret Witter and Peter Vegso at HCI for their faith in me and their vision in putting this book on the stands. I hope sales justify their taking a chance on me and on the unsexy topic of forgiveness.

Finally, and always, I thank Sue, my wife. She is from heaven, as are our three kids, Lucy, now fourteen, Jack, eleven, and Tucker, eight. I had a pretty crazy childhood myself, but thanks to Sue and these three spirited rogues, I am getting to participate at last in the unbeatable joy of happy childhoods. Thank you, God, for allowing us this.

## Part One

# What Is Forgiveness?

# 1

# Forgiveness Is a Gift
# You Give to Yourself

When a well-known sportswriter in Boston died not too long ago, something terrible happened, a terrible something that happens so often that nobody usually comments on how terrible it is. The terrible thing was that a man who had once been a close friend of the sportswriter stayed away from the funeral. The erstwhile friend was still bitter over a disagreement the two of them had had a couple of years before the sportswriter's death. An argument blew up and burned them both. Resentment took root, and like the weed that it is, it grew fast. Soon, what had been a trusting, fun-filled friendship was overrun by an impenetrable thicket of anger and self-justification. Two men who'd been good friends for years became enemies. As so often happens, one of them died before they could find a way to forgive each other and resume the friendship they both had so much enjoyed.

It's hard to find the right word for that situation: sad, silly, tragic, foolish, understandable, spiteful, petty, human, absurd, a waste. In any case, it happens all the time. An action leads to anger, which leads to the end of trust and warmth. Close friends turn into cursed fools. Everybody loses. It is so stupid, so wasteful, so sad, so wrong.

What would it have taken for the sportswriter and his friend to make up? That question gnawed at me enough to start me researching and writing this book. Soon I was going to bed and waking up wondering, *What does it take for any of us to make up with those we can't forgive? What is it about forgiveness that is so difficult?* Even when we know it is in our best interests to do it, we agonize over it.

What does it take to forgive? The diplomatic skills of a secretary of state? A miracle from above? Or is forgiveness simply never to be when the deeds are really bad? Is forgiveness of grievous wrongs a naive idea that only superficial sentimentalists unschooled in the ways of the world still believe in?

On the other hand, might forgiveness be worth a try? If so, why? How can a normal person do it?

Recent research has given us important information about forgiveness. We now have reliable, empirical data, not just our subjective musings. Based on that data, I now know that what happened to the sportswriter and his friend has a practical remedy, as does what happens to the millions upon millions of the rest of us who become stuck in grudges, anger and resentment.

Forgiveness is a remedy we rarely use. As a result, we suffer when we don't need to. That sportswriter and his friend could have made up. Like so many of us, they didn't. Instead they dug in, each convinced of the rightness of his position.

We've all seen this happen. A spat becomes a grudge

becomes a feud becomes a schism. Along with precious heirlooms, parents bequeath to their children resentments they inherited from their parents. Partnerships dissolve over a silly squabble, and great businesses crumble. A murder begets other murders, which beget wars.

Why? What about the remedy? Why don't we use that? Isn't forgiveness better than family feuds and failed businesses and ruined friendships and cycles of murders and wars?

Well, of course it is. But it is a devilishly difficult remedy to apply. It's so hard to use, we'd sometimes rather die than try, especially when the hurt runs deep and has run for a long time. Millions of dead people have shown us their preference to die rather than forgive. You might logically conclude that forgiveness of great crimes is pretty near impossible, especially if the best of your life has been ruined by what someone else has done.

But forgiveness is never impossible. Never. If you manage to do it, you're the one who benefits the most.

Still, we tend not to forgive. We get mad at a close friend, carry a grudge and refuse to attend the funeral when the friend dies. That's the way of the world, isn't it—this silly, silly world, a world in which we're bent on wasting the best that we have? After a fight, instead of making up, each participant furiously details why he is in the right and the other person is a rotten, no-good, dirty rat—even though they loved each other just days before, not to mention the years and years before that.

All of a sudden, for us stubborn humans, being right becomes more important than being close. It becomes more important to justify our case than to make peace. We invest our energies in defaming the other person, the very same person we recently treasured as a dear friend. What's gained by being so stubborn and self-righteous? I'm not sure what's gained, but whatever it is, we defend it with our lives.

In so doing, we can destroy the best of life: friendship and peace. If only we could get better at forgiving, at not taking extreme offense so quickly, at being willing to come back into the room after we have stormed out of it, then we would live longer, happier, less complicated and less foolish lives. We wouldn't waste the best of what we have.

We weren't brought up to be as foolish as we become. Most of us were brought up to forgive. The problem is, no one told us how to do it when we were children, or even why we should. Forgiveness was just one of those "oughtas" we all heard. "You oughta forgive your brother." "You oughta forgive your friend." But since we weren't told how, we had to wait for forgiveness to appear, as if by magic.

Of course, we didn't hold our breaths. We really didn't care very much, because we didn't know why forgiving was such a good thing, other than that parents and teachers and religious people recommended it. While they recommended it, we couldn't help but notice they usually didn't practice it. So we turned to what came to us naturally and was a lot more exciting: holding grudges and seeking revenge.

I have since found out that it is worth learning the act of forgiveness, even though it never comes naturally. Now that I have grown up and become a doctor and actually researched the topic, I have learned a lot. The grown-ups back when I was a kid may not have known the hows and whys of forgiveness, but, like a good night's sleep or a balanced diet, they were right to recommend it. Medically speaking, it is really good for you to forgive. It's much, much better than holding a grudge or seeking revenge. Learning how to forgive ranks near the top of the practical steps you can take to improve your life, your physical health and your emotional health. Furthermore, the price is good; it's free.

It's also freeing. When you forgive, you free yourself from mind-forged manacles. You start to derive benefits as soon as you gain release from the anger and resentment that have held you down.

Among the many health benefits, your blood pressure may go down, your resting heart rate may decrease, your immune system may get stronger, your susceptibility to a heart attack or a stroke may decrease, headaches and backaches and neck pain may abate, your need for medications may diminish, and even your sexual self may gain strength. If this sounds like a lot, it actually isn't anywhere near a complete list of the potential physical benefits of forgiveness.

I haven't even mentioned the emotional benefits. Forgiving lifts your spirits. It makes you feel happier, and it clarifies your thinking. No longer must you carry a lodestone of anger and resentment. The lift returns to your step, and your day does not dawn in a shadow of grievance.

Compared to other measures people take to improve their lives, forgiving is at least as good for you as losing weight, getting the right amount of sleep, taking supplemental vitamins or wearing seat belts. However, as I have mentioned, forgiving is hard to learn to do. We need help.

Unlike most other steps we can take toward a better life,

there isn't much written to offer us help on how to forgive. We find we're still where we were when we were growing up: lots of people recommend forgiving, but they neither tell us how to do it nor do they show us in their own lives.

I want to change that.

Here's good news. However difficult it may be, forgiving is a skill anyone can learn. If you have the desire and are willing to practice, you can learn how to do it, even if you're a stubborn alpha male! While mystery may surround forgiveness, and while magic or grace or luck may propel it, forgiveness is nonetheless a skill that anyone can acquire if they want to. I offer many examples in this book.

❀ ❀ ❀

But first, let me tell you a story about forgiveness that ironically illustrates the dangers of avoiding it. I have a friend in Seattle who hates the man he used to work for. He has hated him for years. He hates him because this man humiliated him, publicly firing him in a hideously demeaning way. To make it worse, my friend had once considered this man his buddy, often going out drinking with him, and to ball games and dinners. Then, out of nowhere, the man turned on my friend and betrayed him, setting him up to take the fall for business mistakes he, not my friend, had made. Ever since then, not a day passed in my friend's life without his thinking of his old boss and filling up with rage. Five years passed.

Late one night, my friend was walking down the street where the man he hated lives. As he drew near the house, the familiar hateful feelings took over. He started to recall the details of what happened, the peremptory e-mail, the refusal to discuss the matter, the public announcement at a motivational rally at work that my friend had "failed to meet expectations in a company committed to meeting expectations," followed by the public request—blared over loudspeakers—that my friend leave the meeting immediately, pick up his belongings at the front desk and never return. Even though the events had happened five years before, it still felt fresh and cruel and wrong.

On this particular night, as he walked past his old boss's house, my friend decided to do something. Nothing major—just something. He had never been able to take any revenge at all, even though he thought about it at least once a day, sometimes more. Although he'd thought about it a lot, he knew he would never do anything big, like hire a hit man to kill his old boss, or cleverly slander him or set him up in an embarrassing tryst. That wasn't my friend's style. But tonight, just for the fun of it, he decided to do something small, something he could easily get away with, something that would do no serious harm but would make him feel good, at least for a minute or two. He decided to do what kids have been doing for years to neighbors they hate. He decided to throw a rock through a window in his old boss's house. It was childish and silly, but the idea felt as good as a strong drink.

Kicking around in the dirt that bordered the sidewalk, my friend looked for the proper stone as this emerging David imagined, if not slaying his own Goliath, then at least bothering him a bit. He told me later that he carefully chose a jagged rock, big enough to do some damage, but small enough to throw hard. Once he found his stone, he wound up and let it fly, rage propelling the rock out of depths of humiliation up into the moonlight toward a corner window of the house of the hated man. For a moment, my friend felt happy. Victorious. Avenged.

But his aim was not David's. Instead of smashing the window, the rock hit a drain pipe right next to the window and ricocheted back. My friend, standing on the sidewalk below, his face eagerly upturned, grinning, expecting to savor this moment, suddenly became the target of the very rock he had thrown. Unable to duck in time, he took the ricochet head-on, as if he had planned to be hit by it all along. The stone struck him on the bridge of his nose, slicing open a cut that took several weeks to heal fully.

He felt foolish, humiliated by this man once again, as he held his arm up to his bleeding nose and hurried home. When he told me about it he laughed, but it was clear that he did not enjoy this bit of laughter. He was the victim of his own hatred.

I wanted to tell him something that Confucius said, but it didn't seem tactful to say it just then. Confucius said, "When you start down the road to revenge, first dig two graves."

If my friend had found a way to forgive his old boss before he took his walk that night, his nose would have been spared, not to mention his pride. But, like all of us sometimes, my friend couldn't forgive.

Most of us don't like to forgive. I don't know anyone who does. It's not fun, and it's difficult. When the stakes are high, forgiving can seem as difficult as performing surgery on yourself, and equally painful. Just thinking about forgiving can make you wince and say, "No way."

Yet in this book I will urge you to try it. Why? Think of my friend who threw the rock. Think how his hatred of his ex-boss owned him and tormented him. Taking a stroll at night, he plotted revenge instead of enjoying the summer breeze. Imagine how many moments in his life had become contaminated with those toxic feelings. Imagine how much time he gave over to nursing his anger and keeping it alive. Through it all, he was the only person who suffered. That is the pitiful irony in being unable to forgive. You are the one who gets hurt.

I wish I could have told my friend how to forgive, but who was I to say what he should do? I was not the person who had been fired, humiliated and betrayed.

I wish I could have told him stories from my own life, or given him the scientific facts I knew from my own medical training about the physical danger of carrying grudges and resentments. I wish I could have told him what I have put into this book, information that could have made his life so much better. I did try, but when I tried, he listened to me no more closely than if I had been a flight attendant announcing how to fasten a seat belt.

In this book, I am going to make another attempt, this time in writing, to explain why and how to forgive.

Perhaps you consider your own case so special, the offense so dire or the situation so complex, that no book or other advice could help. But we all think our own anger is special. The longer you nurse it, the longer you keep it in your heart, the more parasitic it becomes. It grows more powerful as it drains you of your health, gradually turning you into a nasty creature like itself. You feed it with your brooding and pacing and clenching of your teeth. Reliving in your mind what happened to make you so angry, you revive your hurt over and over again, each time refeeling your rage and refining your visions of revenge. Gradually, you ruin your sense of joy in life, which is bad for you in every conceivable way.

To put an end to it, you need a radical cure, a cure that reaches in and takes hold of the parasite of rage and rips it away from what it's sucking on: the walls of your own heart. Forgiveness, not revenge, is the only radical cure.

When you forgive, you cut the parasite from its food supply. Now you can watch it wither and slowly die.

Forgiveness is a gift you give to others, but it also a gift you give to *yourself.*

Question: How can I keep the peace in my friend-ships and minimize potential relationship-ending disputes?

Answer: Listen. Fess up when you are wrong. Tell the truth. Try to imagine yourself in your friend's shoes when you disagree. Don't let problems slide. Never put being right above all else. The most bitter disputes are always between two parties who are "right."

# 2
# Forgiveness Detoxifies
# Hurt and Hatred

**F**orgiveness begins in a bitter place. It begins in words like these: "When you walked out on me, I vowed I would never forgive you."

"When you tricked Dad into signing the business over to you before he died, you knew exactly what you were doing. I will always hate you for that."

"How can I forgive when so many have died? To forgive would be to forget about them. It would be wrong and immoral not to keep my rage alive."

"After all that I did for you, you organized those people into a mob and you manipulated them into turning on me and bringing me down. You are despicable, and I will never forgive you."

"You could have helped me back then, but you just walked right by me. You played it safe and chose not to get involved. Now that I'm on top you want to be my friend? You must be joking. I detest you, your opportunism and all the people you represent."

"There is no way I can ever forgive you. I once loved you, but you have broken my heart."

In words like these—spoken in moments of terrible anguish—forgiveness begins. Forgiveness must build a bridge over pain, often tremendous pain.

Forgiveness starts in hurt, in anger, in disbelief, in confusion. It starts in hatred. It starts in a florid wish for revenge. It starts in bitterness and shock and disappointment. It starts in the fixed belief that you can never, must never and will never forgive this act.

It starts in a lawyer's office, at a funeral, on the side of the road, in a bar, alone in bed in the middle of the night, out fishing, on a deathbed, early one morning, late one night or in the full sun of midday.

Forgiveness starts in pain.

If you are lucky, it ends in peace. Whether you are seeking forgiveness or trying to grant it, you begin in distress, hoping to find your way to a peaceful place. You don't know how to get there, and you know you may never arrive. Indeed, many journeys to forgiveness fail. They get stuck in thickets and thorns of resentment, pride, self-justification and rage.

Whether we are trying to forgive ourselves and overcome guilt, or we are trying to forgive some person or some force that has done us wrong, we begin in one of the darkest, most closed-off places life knows, a place that seems to have no exit.

One question that can help light the way out is this: What do you want your pain to turn into? Do you want it to turn into a grudge, a war, a lawsuit or an endless conflict? Do you want it to turn into suffering for the person who hurt you?

Some people call that justice. Gandhi pointed out the problem with that kind of justice when he said, "If you take an eye for an eye, pretty soon the whole world will be blind." If you want your pain to turn into more pain, then you will never leave the dark place you're in.

If, on the other hand, you want your pain to turn into something else, something positive—like growth, wisdom, peace, health, or the relief of others' suffering or of your own —then revenge is not your best option. As sweet as revenge may seem when you have been hurt, a sweeter, smarter choice is forgiveness.

While revenge grants a seemingly delicious satisfaction, that satisfaction is composed of the very same seductive poisons that led the person who hurt you to hurt you in the first place. Revenge, or what's called retributive justice, simply recirculates the toxins through the bloodstream of humanity from generation to generation. Under the guise of providing relief from pain, revenge does the opposite. Revenge promotes revenge. Back and forth it goes. Like a grim tennis game, vengeance seems to be this world's favorite sport. But this sport only promotes hurt and pain. Ask yourself, is that what you want your pain to turn into? More pain?

Or do you want your pain to transmogrify? To change into something entirely different? Do you want your pain to become, in some marvelous way, a blessing? The way to make that happen is through a mysterious process called forgiveness.

Reaching forgiveness takes guts. It also takes wisdom, patience and imagination. It can be the most complex psychological journey you'll ever take. It is a trip up a narrow grade, against the slope of human nature and against the slope of popular opinion. The mob does not want us to forgive. If you lift up the veil that covers the human mob, you will find a bloodthirsty beast that feeds on vengeance. As a group, we humans crave vengeance; mobs thrive on vendettas. Lonely and brave is the man or woman who stands up against the throng and says, "No more. The blood stops here. I forgive my enemy."

What happens after wrong has been done—by you or to you—is so difficult to untangle because a force field of radioactive emotion surrounds it. This book would be very short if forgiveness were easy. All we would have to do to gain or grant forgiveness would be to say, "I'm sorry," or "You are forgiven," and that would be the end of it.

But as much as we might wish to be forgiven or wish to forgive, forces as strong and ancient as gravity pull us away. We struggle to get there, we imagine we have arrived, but then we are back where we started, stuck in guilt or resentment.

When we have been hurt, or when we have hurt someone else, the cumbersome psychological machinery of retribution cranks up like an awful instrument from the Great Inquisition. The cables of this psychological machinery run deep in our brains and in our cultural history. If there were a set of Newton's Laws for psychology as there is for motion, one of them would surely be: *For every wrong, humans seek an equal and opposite wrong.*

We don't have much equipment to resist this all-but-irresistible force. The only tool we're given to resist it is our will to do so, but we must use that lonely tool, as pitifully inadequate as it might seem to be. By wanting to, we can start to renounce the forces of hatred coiled within us. On the other hand, if you don't want to, you won't forgive. You'll merely forget.

Before you feel justified and comfortable in not wanting to forgive, ask yourself once again, *What do I want my pain to turn into?* As much as you may feel that you want it to turn into the suffering of the person who hurt you, stop and think. Wouldn't your own growth, health and happiness, as well as the betterment of others, be preferable to the suffering of your tormentor? Don't you want to free yourself from the cycle of pain? If your answer is yes, then you want to forgive.

Then the question becomes: How?

On our good days, we forgive each other and ourselves without too much effort. Not just for the big things that rarely happen, but for the little things that happen frequently. Someone lets a door close in your face. A neighbor doesn't clean up after her dog who regularly poops on your walk. A person cuts in front of you in line at the supermarket while pretending not to see you. A doctor doesn't give you the time you need. A friend won't stick up for you when you need him. A spouse gets angry because you forgot to change a light bulb. You get a parking ticket or speak harshly to your children or feel jealous over a friend's good fortune or eat too much. If we could forgive others and ourselves for the petty crimes and misdemeanors we all commit dozens of times every day, think how much positive energy we would free up to do better things in our lives than feel resentment, pursue vengeance or languish in guilt!

But habitual, active forgiveness, the kind of forgiveness that elevates your life and makes you a healthier, happier,

more effective person, does not happen by accident, by reve-
lation or by the mere passage of time.

Forgiveness comes from a decision you made long ago to
live in a certain way. You don't have to be religious; indeed,
many religious people can't forgive anything. You don't have
to be a goody-goody; indeed, many goody-goodies are
secretly nasty. You don't have to become a saint, take special
vows, undergo therapy or get on some medication.

All you really have to do is look for the best in others and
in yourself. When you try to do that, you set forgiveness in
motion.

Let me give you an example. I know a woman, let's name
her Rose, who is a lawyer. One year she decided to run for the
mayor of her city. She was well known and respected in the
community, and the polls showed her taking a huge early
lead. Voters were thrilled to have such a bright, honest, ide-
alistic person entering the field.

As her lead continued to grow, her opponent became desperate. One evening my friend gave a talk at a school where,
during the Q&A, someone asked her if she believed in God.
She said she did, but that she also believed religion and politics didn't mix very well. The next day the student newspaper misquoted her as having said she believed God wanted
her to win the election. Her opponent took this misquote from
the student newspaper, printed it up and plastered it all over
the city.

Her opponent—let's name him Kevin—was just getting
started. He next gave a false story to the city newspaper stat-
ing that Rose had covered up a case of sexual harassment in
her law practice and had also conspired to get charges

dropped against a child molester. There was no truth to either of the stories, but they did their job. Rose lost the election by a few hundred votes.

Although she was devastated and disillusioned, she still had to continue to live in her city. It was her home. But she felt utterly betrayed. Not only had Kevin lied about her, but others in the community, including many of her "friends," had started to avoid her, just in case the allegations against her were true. They didn't want to be seen having anything to do with someone who even *might* be tainted.

Rose had good reason not only to hate her opponent, but to hate humanity in general. She had seen not only the vicious side of one man, but the shameful side of the general public, "friends" who deserted her when she needed them the most.

But Rose was a woman who did not like to live in hateful states of mind, no matter how justified they were. She believed in making the best of whatever happened, and she believed in forgiveness. She happened to be a Christian, but most of the "friends" who deserted her were Christians too.

Being a Christian, Rose had been taught to pray when she was in distress. So she prayed now. She prayed for the ability to let go of her anger and hatred, but it was slow going. She told me that one night as she was driving past the house of one of the people who had abandoned her, she imagined taking one of those rocket launchers she'd seen in movies and shooting a rocket into that house to blow it to smithereens.

She continued to talk with her true friends about her anger. She continued to pray. She tried to empathize with those who had hurt her, which was tough. Whenever she thought of them, she only felt rage.

Gradually, though, she began to see Kevin as a man who had nothing else in his life but his ratings, his political office. She began to see that he *had* to win, and she realized that she didn't. She didn't want victory at any cost. She also saw that the "friends" who deserted her were no worse than people have always been. She was discovering firsthand what she had read about in literature and history: People are, by and large, selfish and weak. The rare few you can depend upon are, well, rare and few.

She also reminded herself that she had not always behaved perfectly in her own life. She knew she needed forgiveness herself. If she couldn't let go of her anger and resentment toward others, how could she hope others could do that toward her?

This process of wrestling within yourself and talking to others, which in Rose's case included talking to God in the form of prayer, is essential in active forgiveness. I describe the process in more detail in later chapters, but this example offers a first look.

Years passed. The hurt ran so deep that the anger took a long time to subside. One day Rose took a walk with a friend, and as she was lamenting what had happened her friend snapped, "Rose, you have just got to let go of this!"

How much easier it is to say that than do it. Rose yearned to get past her anger. She prayed to let it go; she did everything she could think of, but it just wouldn't go, which is how it is when you have been deeply hurt. Your outrage, your feeling of how-*could*-they-have-done-that, does not easily subside, no matter how much you may want it to.

Rose took specific steps to make sure her outrage did not

rule her life while she was wrestling within herself, trying to forgive. She did not leave town. She did not even leave the church where so many of the "friends" who deserted her also worshiped.

In fact, a pivotal event occurred at church. Rose was chalice bearer during Holy Communion one Easter Sunday. As she passed the cup of wine from parishioner to parishioner, whom should she see kneeling before her, awaiting his holy meal, but Kevin, the very man who had slandered and libeled her?

Rose paused. Everything that had happened cascaded through her mind and she felt dizzy. She knew she had to administer the cup, but to him? Of course, to him. She leaned down to Kevin, who kept his head bowed, not making any eye contact. Rose presented the cup to Kevin's lips and let him take his sip of wine as she spoke the designated words of blessing. Then, before moving on to the next parishioner, she squeezed one of Kevin's hands. Only then did he look up at her. She could see his eyes had welled up with tears.

That was as close to an apology as she ever got. But it was enough for her to finally—seven years after the election—let go of the anger and resentment that had so festered within her. Here is how she described to me what happened:

From the point when I became willing to forgive, several weeks after the election, to the experience at the altar on Easter Sunday seven years later, I longed for an apology or for those who had been dishonest and hurtful to open a door to dialogue. I knew that if I were asked to forgive, that I could respond. Of course, forgiveness and healing generally don't occur according to our scripts, and I learned that sometimes it is necessary to take that extra step, like squeezing Kevin's hand at the altar rail, to breach the divide. Now, ten years later, I would appreciate genuine attempts at reconciliation from those who perpetrated the fraud on the public, but the memories are no longer haunting, and only rarely does it all come to mind. I have heard it said that resentment corrodes most the container that holds it. I guess that is why forgiveness is essential to our mental and physical well-being.

It took Rose seven years to reach forgiveness. But think how much better off she was in working toward forgiveness than if she had spent those seven years filing lawsuits (which she considered doing but decided it would cause more pain than good), plotting revenge or simply focusing on hatred. Think how much better off she was than if she had given in to bitterness, or had taken up drugs or alcohol as a way of soothing herself.

A lengthy journey to forgiveness is far better for a person than a lengthy journey to revenge. It is not just the end point that matters, but the process you undergo as you get there.

Question: I'm too embarrassed to call up a former friend and make peace. What can I do to swallow my pride?

Answer: You've already done the hard part. You have acknowledged that it is your pride, not just your friend's problems, that blocks the way.

Now think about this: What does it mean to swallow your pride? What is your pride giving you that swallowing it will take away? It's probably a feeling of safety. As long as you hide behind your pride and keep your distance, you will feel safe and in control.

But if you set aside your pride and approach your friend without that armament, you give up some control and leave yourself vulnerable. What if your friend takes advantage and ridicules you? You will feel doubly hurt. So why bother?

Because you care. And because you are wise. As Samuel Johnson wrote more than two hundred years ago, "To let friendship die away by negligence and silence is certainly not wise. It is voluntarily to throw away one of the greatest comforts of this weary pilgrimage."

The chances are that your friend will put down her pride when you approach her, and you will rekindle a great friendship. Now it will be even stronger, having weathered a hard time. But even if your attempt fails, you will feel better because you will have done what you can do.

# 3

## Forgiveness Sets You Free

To understand forgiveness, you must first understand what forgiveness is not. Forgiveness is not turning the other cheek. Forgiveness is not running away. Forgiving someone does not mean that you condone what the person has done, nor does it mean that you invite them to do it again. It doesn't mean that you don't want the offending person to be punished. It doesn't mean that you forget the offense, nor does it mean that by forgiving you tacitly invite bad things to happen again. It doesn't mean that you won't defend yourself.

So what does it mean? Forgiveness is one of those words that we assume we can define, but when asked we stumble. Before you read on, try it yourself. How would you define forgiveness?

The dictionary can help. My *American Heritage College Dictionary* defines "forgive" as, "To renounce anger or resentment against." It goes back to a Greek root word that means "to set free," as in freeing a slave. Ironically, when we forgive, the slave we free is ourselves. We free ourselves from being slaves to our own hatred.

According to the dictionary definition I just cited, in order to forgive we must renounce resentment or anger. We do not have to forget, ignore or condone anyone or anything. We just have to renounce our anger and resentment. Even doing that may seem impossible, especially if whom or what we are trying to forgive has hurt us deeply. How do you forgive murder, child abuse or any other horrible offense? How is anyone supposed to renounce anger and resentment in cases like those? How do you stop feeling what you are feeling, or at least how do you renounce what you are feeling? And exactly what does that word "renounce" mean?

Turning to the same dictionary, I look up "renounce," and find the following definition: "To reject, disown."

This helps. In order to forgive I am not required to cease to feel anger or resentment, only to renounce anger or resentment, which means to disown my anger and resentment.

This distinction is crucial, not just a nicety of language. One of the chief reasons that people don't try harder to forgive or be forgiven is because they think it is impossible. They think that forgiving means ceasing to feel anger, hurt or the desire for revenge. How can you forgive someone who has murdered your friend, ruined your career, taken away your spouse or hurt one of your children? If forgiveness means that you cease to feel any anger or resentment toward that person, then for most of us forgiveness is indeed impossible—if not immoral—when the injuries are severe.

Forgiveness has therefore taken on a daft quality for many people, or at least a quaintness, as if forgiveness were a sweet old lady—a sweet old idea, one to which we pay our respects but think of as fragile and weak, unable to help us do the heavy lifting of everyday life. For the heavy lifting we believe we need strong young men—ideas that pack a punch, like vengeance, retribution and that great masquerader, justice.

But that is wrong. Forgiveness is much stronger, not to mention much wiser, than vengeance or retribution, and it begets the best kind of justice. Forgiveness is not a sweet old lady but a strong, seasoned veteran of many wars. Forgiveness bears a greater burden than vengeance ever could. Vengeance lets hatred rule you. Forgiveness overrules hatred. Forgiveness is not only stronger; it is much more clever and wise than vengeance or retribution. Forgiveness takes intelligence, discipline, imagination and persistence, as well as a special psychological strength, something athletes call mental toughness and warriors call courage.

If you look back at the definition of forgiveness, you can see why so much more is required of a person to forgive than to take revenge. When you forgive, you renounce anger and resentment. You give up your claim to anger and resentment. You disown those feelings, you repudiate them, you turn your back on them. Above all, you cease to live under their rule. You are consciously, deliberately renouncing your claim to what you probably want more than anything in the world: retribution, vengeance, a chance to get even. Doing this takes immense courage and strength.

But forgiveness does not require that you cease to feel the anger and resentment you so naturally experience. Not at all.

This crucial distinction is what makes forgiveness humanly possible, albeit still strange and difficult.

What does it mean to give up your title to anger and resentment or to refuse to live under their rule? It means that you set yourself free from those feelings. You no longer let those feelings own you; you disown them. When you feel the yoke of hatred start to take you in its grip, you step out. You lift it off. You renounce it. You put on the yoke of love, instead.

When you've been hurt, why on earth would you do this? In order to improve your own life. As Joanna North, a philosopher and renowned expert on forgiveness, put it: "What is annulled in the act of forgiveness is not the crime itself but the distorting effect that this wrong has upon one's relations with the wrongdoer and perhaps with others."

Throughout her writing, North emphasizes how forgiving (or accepting forgiveness) makes people healthier and happier. As she says, "Through forgiveness the pain and hurt caused by the original wrong are released, or at least *they are not allowed to mar the whole of one's being for all time*" (italics mine).

On the other hand, holding onto your title to anger and resentment, as if it were a precious deed of ownership, is like holding onto your title to a polluted pond.

Now, return to what I asked before: If you know why you want to forgive, then how do you do it? How do you stop feeling what you are feeling? It is often not enough just to want to. How do you stop your anger from ruling you?

The definitions point the way. You do *not* have to stop feeling what you are feeling. That's impossible. However, you can refuse to act on those feelings by hurling hand grenades or insults, and you can refuse to welcome those feelings when they hungrily come to your door, hoping to feed on your fantasies of revenge.

Renouncing certain feelings is something we've all learned

how to do. For example, we renounce our aggressive feelings when we are stopped by a traffic cop for speeding. We might feel like punching the cop's lights out, but we renounce those feelings, we do not act on them, we disown them, we repudiate them, we do not let ourselves live under their rule. We continue to feel them; the feelings are still very much with us. We simply renounce their control over us.

I shouldn't say "simply" because such renunciation requires strength, patience and skill. But we manage to do it, *every day,* not only with our aggressive feelings, but also with our sexual feelings, and even our feelings of hunger and thirst or the need to use the bathroom.

When we forgive, we may continue to feel anger and resentment, just as we may continue to feel anger and resentment at the traffic cop who stopped us. But, if we are wise, we put those feelings aside. We do not let them rule our actions.

Furthermore, we try not to welcome the feelings when they skulk back, looking to be nursed. That means when we think of the person who hurt us, we do not give in for very long to the temptation to dream up scenes of revenge or revel in methods of torture. You can luxuriate in imagined scenes of revenge, you can cuddle and nurse your angry feelings, but after a while you risk nursing those feelings into a monster that ends up destroying you, not your enemy.

Let's say you've been betrayed by a coworker, which led to your getting fired from your job. Do you really want to spend parts of the next five or ten years contemplating scenes of this person being humiliated, fired, rejected or in other ways hurt? For a little while, yes, you do. You should; you need to. But for months and years? Wouldn't that mean you gave that person more power over you than was good for you? Wouldn't that mean that the person had achieved a double victory: first by getting you fired, then second by infecting your free time with fantasies of revenge?

Try to think of feelings of anger and resentment as dangerous drugs—useful sometimes in small doses, but highly toxic as regular intake. Try to resist welcoming them into your imagination. They rarely do you good. They often do you serious harm.

When the vengeful feelings creep in, refuse to live under their rule, for your own sake.

Instead, be guided by the principle of love.

This is where forgiveness gets tricky. How can you love, or even like, someone who has hurt you? You naturally feel emotions quite different from love, be they fear, anger, resentment, dislike or even hatred. You cannot control what you feel, any more than you can control the weather.

But you can control what you do with what you feel. You can renounce the rule of anger, resentment and hatred, and subscribe instead to the rule of love. This much you can control. This much you can consciously and deliberately decide to do.

Gradually, as you resist the rule of anger, you can develop empathy for your enemy. There is no one you can't develop something like love for if you know their whole story. I know that sounds like an awful stretch when you are talking about people who have done terrible deeds. In those cases, simply begin by letting the principle of love rule your actions, the principle of love for all humankind, not just love for your friends. Then, gradually try to understand where the evil came from. Try to understand how your enemy, who was once an innocent and loving infant, turned into such a monster. As you understand, your hatred will gradually subside, and in its place something like love will start to grow.

Right alongside, you will grow as well.

# Nine Types of Forgiveness

*Acts of forgiveness vary not only in the magnitude of the wrongdoing involved, but in several other key ways. For example, are you the one seeking forgiveness, or is someone seeking forgiveness from you? Do you acknowledge you have done wrong? Does the person who has wronged you take responsibility for inflicting the hurt? Is he or she sorry?*

*Forgiveness will be more or less difficult to perform depending upon these various conditions. Let me describe nine basic categories in which forgiveness may be sought or granted.*

**Type I:** *You have been wronged. The other person apologizes and seeks forgiveness from you.*

*This situation leads to forgiveness most easily. Of course, if the hurt is deep enough, you may not be able to forgive, even with an apology and attempts at restitution.*

**Type II:** *You have been wronged. The other person does not acknowledge the wrongful act and does not seek forgiveness.*

*It is much more difficult to forgive if the other person does not even acknowledge the wrongdoing, let alone offer an apology. Still, it is in both of your best interests to work your way through the process and reach forgiveness.*

**Type III:** *You have been wronged. You don't know who did it. You don't know whom to blame or whom you might forgive.*

*Let's say your apartment is broken into while you are out and all your valuables are stolen. This happened to me once. Not knowing who did it made the feeling of vulnerability all the more intense. The most important step here is to do all you can to regain your feeling of safety and control.*

**Type IV:** *You have done wrong. You acknowledge what you have done and you seek forgiveness from the other person.*

*This is the reverse of Type I. Depending upon the psychology of the other person, you may or may not find forgiveness. However, by apologizing and making restitution, you have done all that you can do. Even if the other person does not forgive you, you should work on forgiving yourself.*

**Type V:** *You have done wrong. You justify what you have done and do not seek forgiveness.*

*Now we are into the realm of tragedy. King Lear banished the only daughter who truly loved him, did not acknowledge that what he did was wrong and did not seek forgiveness until it was too late. The major reason it is good to study such examples is to help us avoid making the same mistake.*

**Type VI:** *You have done wrong. You acknowledge to yourself that what you have done is wrong, but you do not dare tell anyone or seek forgiveness.*

*This situation brings us into the realm of toxic guilt. The more you keep secret what you did, the more difficult it will be for you to gain absolution or to forgive yourself. It is best to find some safe person, like a doctor or clergy person, and talk it through.*

**Type VII:** *Wrong has been done. All parties involved justify what they have done, and no one seeks forgiveness.*

*Now we are in the realm of world politics. Or local politics. Or family feuds. If we're lucky, a wise diplomat will intervene.*

**Type VIII:** *Wrong has been done. Some people on both sides acknowledge responsibility and seek forgiveness, while others do not.*

*This is, of course, a better situation than Type VII, although if it is a small minority working toward forgiveness, they will likely fail. However, they will triumph by gaining personal integrity and health.*

**Type IX:** *Wrong has been done. It was an act of fate. No one is to blame, but still some people feel guilty and seek forgiveness while others feel angry and seek revenge.*

*For example, let's say you lose a friend to a serious illness. It is the human condition that's to blame, but that doesn't help. And while the human condition is what you need to forgive, that doesn't help much either. The best solution in this situation is to grieve. Express sadness, rather than letting anger take over.*

※　※　※

*You can immediately see that some acts of forgiveness are much more difficult than others. If I bump into you in a busy corridor and I say, "Please excuse me," you will probably have no difficulty forgiving me. On the other hand, if I bump into you and say, "Get out of my way!" then you will probably have a great deal of difficulty in forgiving me. If you get bumped into and knocked to the floor and when you look up no one is there to blame, then you are left with the frustration of having no one to blame, but knowing that someone did you wrong.*

*It is psychologically difficult not to know whom to blame because it challenges our sense of control. The more fate reminds us that we are at its mercy, the more insecure and frightening life becomes. One of the great motivators toward blame and revenge, other than the proverbial balancing of the scales, is that blame and revenge restore the feeling, at least somewhat, that we are in control. Two wrongs may not make a right, but they feel better to the person who suffered the first wrong.*

*This classification of different kinds of forgiveness can help in sorting out forgiveness in your own life and discussing it with others.*

# 4

# Forgiveness Improves
# Your Health

**W**hy should any of us go through all the muck it takes to reach forgiveness? Why not just stay angry, especially when you are in the right?

The answer is simple and powerful. You should learn to forgive for exactly the same reason you should quit smoking, work to lower your cholesterol, go on a diet to lose weight or take up exercise to control your blood pressure. Forgiving improves your life by improving your physical and emotional health and by increasing your chances of living longer. If that isn't enough reason to learn to forgive, consider that living in anger and resentment can be as bad for you as smoking cigarettes or having high blood pressure or an elevated level of cholesterol. In other words, anger and resentment can kill you.

Let yourself be guided by your answer to the question, "What do I want my pain to turn into?" If your answer is more pain, only this time for someone else, take a moment and reflect. Do you really mean that? Is the best part of you speaking when you say that? If you still say yes, let me try to persuade you otherwise.

Scientific studies show that angry, resentful people have heart attacks more frequently than those who forgive more naturally. People who harbor anger and resentment are more likely to erupt and lose control, and they are more prone toward violence. They are more likely to self-medicate with alcohol or other drugs, and they are less able to make positive human relationships that last.

On the other hand, what might be the benefits of holding a grudge or exacting revenge? They are similar to the benefits of smoking cigarettes or taking drugs: short-term pleasures with long-term penalties.

Even if we manage to get the revenge we seek, which we usually don't, the benefits are not nearly as delicious as we imagined they would be. Revenge is a pleasure that is vastly overrated. Our desire for revenge can turn into a craving, often to the point of an insane passion (think of President Nixon or Captain Ahab). We imagine that exacting revenge will somehow make things right. We hope that revenge will end our pain and bring "closure"—the misleading word that is so often used in situations where revenge is sought as a remedy for injustice. As we imagine vengeance in our minds, we feel good. We imagine that it will "close" the open wound. When we are wronged, we yearn for resolution or "closure."

But when we actually live it out—when in fact we get our revenge—it isn't what we imagined it would be. Rarely does it close any wound, because pain does not heal pain. Loss does not cure loss. Rather than closure, revenge gives deceptive satisfaction that can't free us from the angry, aching place we inhabit. And revenge deepens our involvement in hatred.

Furthermore, revenge doesn't clean up the situation. Just

the opposite. It makes more of a mess. Revenge does not bring back the dead, nor undo the wrong, nor repair the fracture. It just breaks more bones. Revenge leaves in its stinking wake more bad feelings, and more people wanting more revenge, thus intensifying the conflict, spewing forth more people with more passionate reasons to perpetuate it.

Aside from being dangerous, a vengeful heart is like bad breath; it is unpleasant to be near someone who has it. You can sense it when you are with one of those people who is raging inside. Anger emanates from them like a foul odor. You don't want to get too close.

Such people collect injustice. They search for it, and they feed their inner anger-monger with it. They are never so pleased as when they are enraged, which usually makes for a mean, unhappy life.

But in less extreme cases, is forgiving still better for you than staying angry or getting even? Usually, it is. Not only physically and psychologically, but even strategically. Let me give you an example of what I mean.

I know a man who is a wealthy real estate developer; we'll call him Hal. He is a very powerful man in the Midwest, and he loves making deals. When I asked him about forgiveness in the business world, I was expecting to hear stories of sharks and how you must eat or get eaten. Instead, he told me the following anecdote.

One day a woman who worked as an accountant for him stole some files and went to a competing firm across town. Unbeknownst to Hal, she had made a secret deal with the competing firm that if she could deliver certain key information that would help the firm take business from Hal, they would give her a better-paying job. What they did not know was that she had stolen the files.

Once the true story emerged, Hal had an airtight case for a giant lawsuit. His colleagues and most of his attorneys salivated at the thought of demolishing the other firm in court, but Hal had another idea. He invited a representative of the other firm to his office. The man arrived, briefcase in hand, looking as if he were about to be executed. Fully believing that Hal was about to blast him, he tried to take the high ground by saying right away, "There is no excuse for what happened. We had no idea all her information came from stolen files. We are ready to make appropriate restitution."

Hal interrupted. "Look," he said, "this whole thing didn't cost me all that much money, and I really would rather spend our time here now thinking up a way we could make a lot more money together, rather than laying out the grounds for a lawsuit. What do you say?"

Hal told me the term "double-take" was invented for how this fellow, Lou, reacted to what he said. He literally reacted twice, with a gulp and a blink, before he finally said, hoarsely, *"You don't want to sue us?"*

Hal, who played on the offensive line at his midwestern college's football team, was a huge man who spoke softly but laughed loud. I can hear him laughing now as he described to me the look of total disbelief on the man's face. "I told him, no, I didn't want to sue. Suing isn't fun, and I hate to feed lawyers. We worked it out in a minute. He gave me back the files my accountant had stolen, and we spent the rest of the time cooking up a deal that turned out to make us both a lot more money than was involved in the other thing. Funny thing, I made friends with Lou. He left his firm a couple of years later to go out on his own, and now he's ended up working with me."

"But Hal," I asked, "weren't you worried that word would get out that you were a pushover?"

"That's what the lawyers were telling me. I think it's all bull. People *know* I'm not a pushover. I don't need to prove it. That's for the Mafia or the movies. I mean, what is this 'word' that's going to get out? That I made more money by not suing than I would have if I had sued? If that word gets out, that's fine with me."

"I don't know business, Hal," I went on, "but I thought you guys had to be pretty ruthless."

Hal laughed again. "What we have to do is make money. Not waste time suing people. Sure, there are times when you need to sue. But most of the time you're better off making a deal."

Making a deal. That's the business equivalent of forgiving, of letting go of anger and resentment. It's better than suing, most of the time. As Abraham Lincoln said, "I have destroyed my enemies by making them into my friends." That is exactly what Hal did.

Forgiving makes strategic sense, and not just in business. Everywhere.

Look at divorces. Look at custody battles. As a child psychiatrist, I look with horror on the madness of these proceedings every day. Not only are they mad, they are tragic, as children suffer permanent damage resulting from their parents' inability to make a deal, to let go of anger and resentment, to forgive.

Everywhere you look, you can find reasons to forgive. Not

just high-minded, moral reasons, but practical reasons based in self-interest.

"Oh, c'mon," you might object. "Revenge runs the world, from playgrounds to corporations. You better be able to get even, or you'll get destroyed."

Well, revenge does run the world and has run the world for as long as people have been able to take offense and try to get even. It is a force that has destroyed billions of lives, but it remains a force that most people cannot resist. It defines the moral code most people actually follow, far outstripping such quaint competitors as mercy, love or understanding.

But even if forgiveness is good for people, you might protest, forgiveness isn't practical. Forgiveness itself can be dangerous. You leave yourself open to attack. You may think that forgiveness is really just reserved for fools, cowards and saints most of the time.

At first glance, perhaps. But take a closer look. Think of Hal.

The real reason people do not forgive more often is not that revenge makes more sense than forgiveness. Revenge is frankly more fun. Revenge, or even just fantasies of revenge, are like getting drunk or pigging out. Forgiveness—the renouncing of anger and resentment—is like going on a diet. It's better for you, but it's far more difficult than giving in to your primal desires, whether the desire is to pig out on food or on fantasies of revenge.

You may still not be convinced. Does any solid research prove the benefits of forgiveness? Indeed, a lot of research does.

The health benefits of forgiveness have been proven often. In fact, research into forgiveness has become a hot topic in the academic community in the past decade. The first national conference on forgiveness ever held at a university campus was convened in 1995 by Robert Enright, professor of education psychology at the University of Wisconsin in Madison. Archbishop Desmond Tutu led off the conference, and a series of scientific presentations on this previously neglected topic followed his talk.

In addition, Dr. Fred Luskin has started an institute at Stanford called the Stanford University Forgiveness Project, which, similar to Professor Enright's group in Wisconsin, is doing pioneering research into forgiveness, a subject that used to be only for sermons, not for scientific research.

Even before the recent research, we have long known that forgiveness is better for you than holding a grudge.

The most basic, proven reason is that chronic anger and resentment constitute a toxic form of stress. We have been reading for decades now about the harmful effects of bad stress. (I use the term "bad stress" or "toxic stress" to differentiate it from stress in general. Life necessarily includes stress, like pumping blood throughout the body or maintaining your posture against gravity. What kills us too young is not ordinary life stress, but toxic or bad stress.)

Toxic stress leads to a host of medical and psychological problems. Even if you have been badly wronged, you are usually better off finding a way to let go of your anger and resentment, justifiable though they may be.

Let me give an example. I have a friend whose neighbor poisoned his dog because she didn't like its incessant barking. She had complained many times to the town, but the animal officer had finally told her that he had done all he could do, and that dogs do bark. She had complained to my friend, and he had told her that he would do his best to keep the dog inside most of the time, where the barking didn't matter. None of this appeased my friend's neighbor, who was an embittered woman, the victim of much misfortune in her own life. When my friend discovered his beloved dog dead, an autopsy showed rat poison as the cause of death. My friend knew whom to blame, but he had no proof.

What was he to do? Enter into a vendetta with this woman? Sue her? Lodge a complaint against her? Bring her to justice? Or maybe throw stones at her windows in the middle of the night?

He certainly had good reason to be angry with her, even to hate her, but what good was that going to do him?

He wanted to put the bad feeling behind him, but how? He loved his dog, and he hated what his neighbor had done.

Here was a set-up for chronic anger and resentment. Every time he looked at his neighbor's house, and every time he thought of his dog, he had reason to rage inside. He had reason to play dirty tricks on his neighbor. He had reason to hate her.

Hating her would only hurt him, though. It could do all the bad things we know toxic stress can do, from increasing the risk of a heart attack to giving him back or joint pain, causing headaches, elevating his blood pressure, and/or reducing the effectiveness of his immune system.

What's more, hating her couldn't bring back the dog. Taking revenge on her couldn't make him miss his dog any less.

My friend was wise enough to see all this. He could see that revenge would only prolong pain, so he set about forgiving his neighbor. It was difficult, as she wouldn't speak to him and of course would not apologize for having done something she never admitted doing.

Forgiving someone who has wronged you and has not apologized is difficult. An apology makes it much easier, but to be wronged and receive no apology is common. When you have been unjustly fired, the boss who fired you does not apologize. When you are betrayed in love, the offending person rarely apologizes. When someone steals from you, they don't leave a note of apology. When someone cuts you off in traffic, he flips you the bird, not an apology.

Life often puts us in the situation my friend was in, of having to find a way to get past anger and resentment without the help of an apology.

If my friend had taken revenge on his neighbor, he would have entered her spiteful game, a game that had long ago taken over her entire life. Because she couldn't get past the bad fortune that had befallen her over the years, she had given in to hatred as a way of life. My friend did not want to do that.

His motivation to forgive did not come from the medical facts about the damage toxic stress can do—although, being a doctor, he knew those facts. His motivation was that he didn't like how he felt when he was consumed with anger and resentment. He knew such a feeling was bad for his health; but more than that, he just didn't like how it made him feel about himself or about life.

Instead of focusing on the evil deed the woman had done or focusing on the woman herself, he set about grieving the loss of his dog. He thought about his dog, cried about his dog, smiled at memories of his dog and put a photograph of his dog on his desk.

He also allowed himself to entertain some vengeful fantasies toward his neighbor. He just didn't revel in them or act on any of them. He would bring his attention back to what he had lost: his dog. The more he talked about his dog, the more he grieved. And the more he talked about his neighbor with his friends—not in a gossipy way, but in an earnest way—the more his anger subsided and was replaced by empathy. "She is a miserable old woman, and I feel sorry for her," he said to me. Not the words of a hateful man.

My friend was able to overrule the natural tendency to get even. In doing so, he was able to preserve his own good feeling about himself and his life, and to grieve the dog he had lost. No amount of suffering he could bring upon his hateful neighbor would have brought back his dog. It only would have continued the cycle of pain.

Beyond its benefits for an individual, forgiveness is good for groups—families, for example. Most families are riddled with grudges. Siblings feud with one another, while one or two brave souls try in vain to bring peace. Fathers feud with their children, while mothers try in vain to find a better way for everybody to get along. Gatherings at holidays and birthdays and other supposedly happy moments become poisoned with old arguments and resurrected hurts.

Forgiveness is good for businesses and all other organizations. Whether a corporation; a church, synagogue or other religious group; a hospital; a school or university department; or any group whatsoever, forgiveness increases communication, reduces toxic emotions, and enhances the life and work of the organization. Lack of forgiveness does precisely the opposite.

You can make forgiveness happen. As Professor Enright says in the title of one of his books, *Forgiveness Is a choice*. His research reinforces the fact that if you decide that you want to, the chances are good that you can forgive just about anything.

Forgiveness is a skill that improves with practice. Again, this is a tested fact, not just conjecture. Enright and others have shown that people who seriously practice forgiveness get better and better at it.

Forgiving is not the same thing as giving in. You do not become a victim when you learn to forgive. Just the opposite. You cease to be a victim. You triumph over hatred, while the person who carries a grudge becomes his own victim.

Question: My father died last summer not long after a huge argument. How can I forgive myself and get rid of the guilt I feel?

Answer: Your mind is playing a trick on you. The trick is a commonly known fallacy in logic that rhetoricians labeled long ago. They called it *post hoc, ergo propter hoc*. That Latin phrase means "after which, therefore because of which." If one event follows another event in time, we may mistakenly conclude that the first event caused the second event. For example, if you drink orange juice in the morning and get sick in the afternoon, you might conclude that the orange juice made you sick, without considering other possible causes.

Our unconscious minds fall for this trick all the time. The unconscious actually believes that "after which" does indeed mean "because of which." This thought is one basis for superstition. If you shoot a good round of golf when you are wearing a certain pair of socks, you may never change those socks again until you shoot a bad round. You know the socks don't make any difference, but your unconscious doesn't buy it, so you consciously defer to irrational wishes and refuse to wash or change your socks.

In the case of superstitions, the consequences are usually trivial. But in the example posed by this person's question, the consequences of buying into the logical fallacy are dire indeed. You have a fight with your father. Before you make up, he dies. You know you didn't kill him, but your unconscious doesn't know that. So you find yourself condemning yourself with guilt. You take it a step further and say to yourself that even if your anger didn't kill your father, the forgiveness you could have offered would have made life better for you both; now that he is gone, however, it is too late. You condemn yourself, and guilt wracks your brain.

You should use reason and remind yourself that you did not kill your father. If you can't convince yourself of this bit of truth, talk to your spouse, a friend or a therapist.

You need to grieve not only your father's death, but also your chance to make up with him while he was alive. Forgiving yourself means that you give up on your hope that the past will be different. The argument with your father will never be resolved, at least not on this Earth. You need to grieve the loss of that chance, get angry over it, cry over it, then put it aside.

# 5

# Forgiveness Is Brave

**M**ost of us aren't good at seeking forgiveness or granting it. Any interaction that involves forgiving makes most of us feel awkward.

We may be good at getting angry when we need to, but not at getting to forgiveness. Although we urge our children to forgive, most of us can't teach them how to do it because we don't know how to do it ourselves. Forgiveness sits up on our mantelpieces like an antique weather vane, a lovely relic that thoughtful people admire, but even those who admire it don't bring it down and use it as a tool in everyday life. It is too fragile to bear the winds of real life.

To tell the truth, we don't know why we should use that old relic. After all, why should we forgive? Forgiving feels weak, like betraying ourselves or whoever was wronged, like giving up or giving in. It feels puny, and as disheartening as defeat. Forgiving can feel wrong, even immoral.

Cynthia Ozick, essayist and fiction writer, pointed out the immorality of forgiveness when she wrote, "Forgiveness is pitiless. It forgets the victim. It negates the right of the victim to his own life. It blurs over suffering and death. It drowns the past. It cultivates sensitiveness toward the murderer at the price of insensitiveness toward the victim."

You might agree with Cynthia Ozick and scorn certain acts of forgiveness.

But even if you disagreed with Ozick and actually wished you could forgive a heinous crime, could you? Or do you have to be a saint to do that? If one person can forgive murder, where does that leave someone like me, who has trouble forgiving the guy who cuts me off in traffic? I don't offer noble reasons for my refusal to forgive, as Cynthia Ozick does when she champions the rights of the victim. I am just a petty, selfish man who will curse at the driver who cuts me off for no better reason than that the driver annoyed me. How can flawed people like me ever forgive anyone for anything? Furthermore, we might add, jutting our jaws, *why should we?*

It feels better to hold fast to pride and call it principle. It feels better, maybe even heroic, to carry anger and resentment with you to your grave, rather than taking the risk of forgiving.

Dostoyevsky described this attitude in *The Brothers Karamazov:*

> Is there in the whole world a being who would have the right to forgive and could forgive? I don't *want* harmony. From the love of humanity, I don't want it. . . . I would rather remain with my unavenged suffering and unsatisfied indignation, even if I were wrong. Besides, too high a price is asked for harmony; it goes beyond our means to pay so much to enter on it. And so I hasten to

give back my entrance ticket. . . . It's not that I don't accept God, Alyosha, only I most respectfully return Him the ticket.

Forgiveness often founders on the rocks of such an attitude. For example, Henry Clay Frick and Andrew Carnegie, two of the giants in American industry in the early twentieth century, were close friends when they were young, but became archenemies during their final decades. One day Carnegie sent a messenger to Frick asking if the two of them might meet face-to-face and work out their differences, as they were both growing old and their time was running out. Frick read the message and abruptly sent the messenger back to Carnegie with the following charge: "Tell Mr. Carnegie that I will meet with him in hell."

The stakes were probably higher between Frick and Carnegie than they are between you and whomever you are on the outs with these days. But I wonder if the psychology isn't approximately the same. I can all but see Frick swelling with pride, imagining himself the heroic captain going down with his ship—namely, his principles—as he rebuffed Carnegie's invitation. Even though his curt message acknowledged mutual blame—they *both* were going to hell—reconciliation was out of the question. He wouldn't even meet with Mr. Carnegie to discuss it.

My sense is that Frick didn't dare. Far from being heroic or brave, Frick in my mind may have been cowardly. He was afraid to forgive, afraid to feel vulnerable, afraid to own up and open up, afraid of his own remorse and his own tender, embarrassing, vulnerable feelings. How much easier to grandly dismiss Carnegie's invitation with the blustering rebuke, "I'll meet him in hell."

Can't you imagine yourself saying that to your spouse as he or she knocks on your door after a really nasty fight? Sure, you're not a titan of industry, but we are all titans of pride and vengeance when we fight with others, especially those we love. "Sweetheart," your spouse might entreat you at the door, "let's talk and make up."

And you, from behind your closed door and with your hard heart, take great relish as you proclaim, "I'll see you in hell." It feels safer to reject the offer than to open the door and let down your guard.

But even as you say it, you know you are chickening out. You know you have just set the course of human civilization back a notch. You know you have not lived up to what you'd like, for example, your children to live up to. You have not been a hero; you have been a selfish, proud fool.

How can anyone move past such selfishness and pride? It is such an unhuman idea to let off the hook someone who has done you wrong. Anger and revenge seem to make much more sense. They're what we humans *do*.

Forgiveness stops the action; it is anticlimactic; it is dull. Can you imagine if Hamlet had said to his stepfather, "Oh, don't worry, big guy, it's okay. Let's get on with life"? Or if Othello had said, "My jealous rage is so lame. I love Desdemona and I will forgive her anything."? The plays would have been flops. Hamlet and Claudius and Desdemona and Othello would have survived, but the plays would have perished.

However, the plays live. Shakespeare got life right. He

knew people. Most people don't forgive, at least not until it is too late. Rage and resentment come as naturally to us as scratching an itch or swatting a fly. We can hardly resist rising up in anger when we are wronged. How good it feels to swell with indignation. How necessary and even heroic it seems to strike back and get even. After all, it's a dog-eat-dog world. If you don't eat, you get eaten.

Forgive? Please. Save it for sermons. It is just not a practical strategy. It is a pretty idea, but it withers in the heat of real life. If you don't take revenge, you'll be taken advantage of. No one will care how virtuous you are; you'll lose in the game of life. Forgiveness is for suckers and sentimentalists.

As if all that weren't enough to trash forgiveness, forgiveness hurts as well. When you forgive, you must give up hardwon, highly prized possessions, like rage and resentment. For most people, giving away a large sum of money is easier than letting go of rage and resentment. Anger provides meaning, structure, direction and motivation in your life. Letting go of something as powerful as that hurts like the devil.

But letting go is worth doing simply because it is the best thing to do. Most of us disregard a vital truth: When you hate, you are the person who gets hurt.

Forgiving has much in common with grieving. Both are hard to do and can feel bad, but both improve our physical, emotional and spiritual health. Both draw upon deeply painful feelings, feelings we'd rather ignore and avoid. Lots of us shy away from forgiving and grieving, because both can be so painful. But if you do not learn how to forgive and grieve, you are the one who will pay. Oddly enough, if ''' do not learn to do this puzzling, stupid, strange,

difficult act called forgiving (as well as grieving), you will suffer in many, many ways throughout your life. Your relationships will suffer, your work will suffer, and your physical
health will suffer. Yet while most people have acknowledged
the importance of grieving, we have all but given up on
forgiveness.

Experts tell us how much grieving matters. Psychiatrists
have long recognized the existence of what is called a
"delayed grief reaction." If someone close to you dies, and
you feel too upset to talk about it and to grieve, it is likely that
a year or two later you will fall into a depression and not
know why. The grief you didn't feel back then has caught up
with you, and is taking its toll upon you now.

Something similar can happen if you do not forgive. As
you continue to hold a grudge and to feel angry, you become
more cynical, less trusting, less hopeful, more irritable and
generally less effective in all aspects of your life. We could call
this a "delayed forgiveness reaction." Anger tends to dominate your mind, and you become less pleasant to be with, as
well as less effective in all that you do, because your mental
energy is being siphoned by the object of your hatred. The
greater the injury you have been unable to forgive, the
greater price you pay and the more it preoccupies you, sucking dry your mental energy. You become demonic, like
Captain Ahab, single-minded in your selfish, self-destructive
pursuit of revenge.

While we have many public forums, ceremonies, rituals,
monuments and works of art that promote and encourage
grieving—from the obituaries in the newspaper to funerals,
wakes, sitting shiva and visiting gravesites regularly;

headstones and monuments; the vast array of painting, music, poetry, sculpture and dance devoted to helping promote the grieving process—we honor very little that helps promote the process of forgiveness.

The Jewish faith has Yom Kippur; Christians have a phrase in the Lord's Prayer, "Forgive us our trespasses, as we forgive those who trespass against us"; but as a society we do not encourage forgiveness very much because forgiveness baffles us. We don't know how to fit it in as a regular part of life, the way we fit in anger or revenge or grief. So forgiveness remains a nice idea, but a rare practice.

In fact, instead of encouraging forgiveness, society has done just the opposite. Starting thousands of years ago, we built a massive legal machinery devoted to helping people seek vengeance and retribution. We honor this system in its minutest details and in its grandest claims; in its name we put people in jail, even put them to death. We have professions devoted to the maintenance of this system. Through lawsuits, criminal prosecutions, and the processes of enforcement and punishment, we spend huge sums and many hours in getting even with those who have done us wrong. On the other hand, I have never heard of a person hiring a lawyer to sue someone for forgiveness.

As strange, painful and difficult as it is, forgiveness is also sweet, but in a different way than revenge. It is a more mature sweetness than the sweetness of revenge. It is like the sweetness of a sigh at good-bye, or the sweetness of a bonfire in autumn, a sweetness that you savor like a conquered fear as you grow older.

How can we learn to do it? First, by wanting to.

Forgiveness comes from wanting to forgive—in principle—then trying to do it. It comes from talking about your pain over and over again, somehow finding safety from the other person, then finding the humanity in the other person and acknowledging imperfection in yourself.

Forgiveness also derives from insight, from knowing that when you hold a grudge, you hurt yourself. Or, as it was put in the Gospel of John, "If you forgive the sins of any, they are forgiven; if you retain the sins of any, they are retained." They are retained in the energy fields of life, in all of us, but most especially they are retained not in the hated person but in the person who will not or cannot forgive.

This is more a medical fact than a moral precept. When you hold hatred, it grows and spreads within you like a wild, undifferentiated tumor. Don't you know people who are slowly dying from metastatic anger? I certainly do.

Forgiveness can shrink the tumor and finally cure the cancer. Another tumor may appear, but then the cure of forgiveness can work again.

Forgiveness begins by choosing to do the only thing we humans can do to free ourselves from the damage done by evil, namely to forgive it. Forgiveness begins in refusing to react as an automatic, reflex-driven human, and choosing instead *somehow* to counteract the human reflex. Hannah Arendt wrote as follows in *The Human Condition:*

> Forgiveness is the exact opposite of vengeance, which acts in the form of re-acting against an original trespassing, whereby far from putting an end to the consequences of the first misdeed, everybody remains bound

to the process, permitting the chain reaction contained in every action to take its unhindered course. In contrast to revenge, which is the natural, automatic reaction to transgression and which because of the reversibility of the action process can be expected and even calculated, the act of forgiving can never be predicted; it is the only reaction that acts in an unexpected way and thus retains, though being a reaction, something of the original character of action. Forgiving, in other words, is the only reaction which does not merely re-act but acts anew and unexpectedly, unconditioned by the act which provoked it and therefore freeing from its consequences both the one who forgives and the one who is forgiven. The freedom . . . of forgiveness is the freedom from vengeance, which encloses both doer and sufferer in the relentless automatism of the action process, which by itself need never come to an end.

Forgiveness originates in the part of each of us that yearns more for an end to foolish suffering and death than for the specious satisfaction of getting even. Unless we extricate ourselves from the cycle of vengeance, *"the relentless automatism of the action process, which by itself need never come to an end,"* unless we actively oppose the cycle of returning hurt with hurt, evil with evil, we remain like subjects in a psychology experiment, predictably doing the same destructive deed over and over again, even when we can see that doing it leads to our own ruin. To get out of the experiment, to rise above the level of a rat's brain, we must look to the unprogrammable part of us that has the autonomy, ingenuity and guts to overrule human nature. We must use the few blessed neurons we've got that are able somehow to orchestrate what feels, at times, impossible: an act of forgiveness.

Forgiveness draws upon a remote and hard-to-reach kind of wisdom, a wisdom that can seem distant and inaccessible.

Because of the distance of the message, we often don't hear it. We ignore the voice of forgiveness because it is too faint or too strange. We dismiss it as being unhuman, not of this world. And we're right. The voices we can easily hear, the loud, intelligible, worldly voices, say "Fight!" "Demand justice!" "Get even!"

But if we strain our ears and listen, we can hear, through the din about revenge, wise voices urging us to use life's time well while we still can. As we listen, those strange, faint voices can build into a clear and penetrating chorus, unmistakable in its refrain: "Forgive, forgive, forgive."

If we will but listen and hear and act, before it is too late.

Question: What do you do when you ask someone to forgive you for something you said, and they never respond? A couple of years ago my happy-go-lucky and lovable brother met a woman, Renee, whom he married one year later. Renee resented our close-knit family (she never got along with her only sister) and clearly had some greedy tendencies. Over the course of a few months, my brother appeared to succumb to her style and became insensitive, selfish and nasty to my parents, especially if they showed any confusion about his behavior. It was like she reprogrammed him. It was so hard to see my parents crying days and weeks before his wedding. We never thought he'd marry such a person. So being the oldest sibling and subsequently feeling like God's deputy, I told him he was brainwashed and acting like a jerk. Of course he took offense, and a year later I apologized in a nice letter (he wouldn't take my calls). When I saw him this summer, he avoided speaking with me. Now I feel really angry that he doesn't value the relationship enough to get it back on track. Should I keep pursuing reconciliation or just forget about it?

**Answer:** There is an old saying, "No good deed goes unpunished." You are getting punished now for trying to help fix a difficult situation. This happens in families all the time. It is very sad.

But don't give up. Try to think strategically. You know yourself and your brother and his wife better than I do, obviously, so you have a better idea of what approach will work.

You want to be careful not to set up a reverberating circuit of anger and resentment between you and your brother, and whatever other members of the family are clued in (which usually means just about everybody).

The anger and resentment will only bind you to each other in a toxic way. As I see it, to forgive someone means to release yourself from the anger and resentment you feel toward the other person. Once you do that, the toxicity you carry subsides.

How do you do that? I think you have to grieve the loss of your brother. All your anger and resentment may be covering a deeper sense of sadness and loss you and other members of your family are feeling. Your brother may also be feeling this sadness as well. But as long as a fight is going on, no one needs to sense the sadness underneath. This is why families, not to mention nations, can fight for generations on end: to avoid the sadness of life.

I think you should look at the possibility that you may have lost the brother you knew and loved. If that's the case, you have to accept it and grieve that loss. Then, and only then, can you let go of the anger and resentment you are feeling toward him and his wife. Your anger is really your attempt to stay attached to him.

Reconciliation may come, later, down the line. A person like you will never stop loving your brother, so there is always the chance of reconciliation. However, you do not want to let yourself be served up as the sacrificial sibling in what can be some pretty cruel family dynamics.

I admire your loving nature. I admire your reaching out to your brother. I understand the hurt you feel at being snubbed by him. My suggestion is to feel the sadness, rather than just the anger; to grieve; and then to wait and see if the brother you once knew reappears.

# How Forgiving Are You?

## A Self-Assessment Quiz

The following quiz offers a rough gauge as to how naturally inclined you are to forgive. Before you take the quiz and consider the meaning of your results, remember how I've defined forgiveness in this book. Being forgiving does *not* mean that you are passive, that you are a victim, that you condone wrongdoing, that you are a pacifist, or that you are weak and afraid to assert yourself or hold firm to a principle that matters to you.

By "forgiving" I simply mean how *inclined* and *able* you are to renounce anger and resentment when you want to, and to grow and help others in the process.

"Inclined" refers to your belief system. In other words, how much of a positive value do you put on forgiveness, defined as renouncing anger and resentment, and transforming yourself and others in the process?

"Able" refers to your emotional capability, your personal psychology. How hard is it for you to renounce anger and resentment?

This quiz should give you a good idea of where you stand along those lines.

Respond to each statement on the self-assessment quiz according to a 5-point rating scale, from 1 to 5. A rating of 1 means you strongly disagree with the statement, while a rating of 5 means you strongly agree with the statement. The ratings are summarized as follows:

1 = Strongly disagree
2 = Disagree
3 = In the middle; partly agree, partly disagree
4 = Agree
5 = Strongly agree

_____   1. An eye for an eye and a tooth for a tooth is a sound guiding principle in life.

_____   2. If you do not take revenge upon people who hurt you, they will take further advantage of you.

_____   3. Nonviolence is an unrealistic policy.

_____   4. I believe children should be raised to get even with others so that they will not be taken advantage of in life.

_____   5. There are people in my life whom I would like to forgive but know that I never will.

_____   6. I tend to hold grudges.

_____   7. I intentionally intimidate people.

_____   8. I am not interested in becoming more forgiving because it will only get me into trouble.

_____   9. Good fences make good neighbors.

_____   10. I am in favor of the death penalty.

_____   11. I approve of taking innocent lives if the cause is just.

_____   12. Loving my enemies is a preposterous idea.

_____   13. I am as forgiving a person as I want to be.

_____   14. Nice guys finish last.

_____   15. When I have been hurt, it is very important to me to get even.

_____   16. If someone embarrasses me in public, I can't rest until I have taken revenge.

_____ 17. I need to be in control all the time.

_____ 18. I do not have much of a sense of humor.

_____ 19. I have a problem with overuse of alcohol.

_____ 20. I have a hard time rolling with the punches.

_____ 21. My parents were not good at forgiving.

_____ 22. I never had many friends growing up.

_____ 23. I feel that people will take advantage of me if I let them.

_____ 24. Reading these statements does not stir any feelings up in me.

_____ 25. I scorn people who walk away from a fight.

_____ 26. I am a proud person.

_____ 27. We need more prisons and stiffer penalties for those who break the law.

_____ 28. Any child who commits murder should be tried as an adult.

_____ 29. Retributive justice is a better policy than restitutive justice. (In other words, it makes more sense to punish criminals than to try to rehabilitate them.)

_____ 30. Mercy for the perpetrator amounts to scorn for the victim of the crime.

_____ 31. Turning the other cheek is a foolish idea.

_____ 32. Negotiating is just a fancy way of wimping out.

_____ 33. I was brought up to settle scores, not make peace.

_____ 34. I feel shame when I apologize.

_____ 35. It's a dog-eat-dog world.

_____ 36. I always know when I am in the wrong.

_____ 37. I have a hair-trigger temper.

_____ 38. Humility is not my long suit.

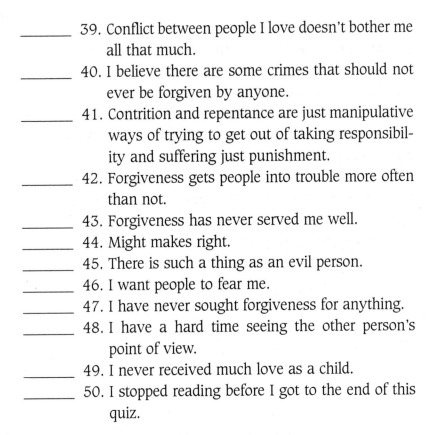

_____ 39. Conflict between people I love doesn't bother me all that much.

_____ 40. I believe there are some crimes that should not ever be forgiven by anyone.

_____ 41. Contrition and repentance are just manipulative ways of trying to get out of taking responsibility and suffering just punishment.

_____ 42. Forgiveness gets people into trouble more often than not.

_____ 43. Forgiveness has never served me well.

_____ 44. Might makes right.

_____ 45. There is such a thing as an evil person.

_____ 46. I want people to fear me.

_____ 47. I have never sought forgiveness for anything.

_____ 48. I have a hard time seeing the other person's point of view.

_____ 49. I never received much love as a child.

_____ 50. I stopped reading before I got to the end of this quiz.

Now, add up the numbers you have given to each question. The lowest possible score is 50. The highest possible score is 250. The higher your score, the less naturally inclined you are to forgive.

No matter how high your score, you can still learn to forgive if you want to. Your conscious mind can overrule your natural tendencies. Indeed, the process of doing just that is what we call civilization.

Here is one way of interpreting your results:

Score 50–75: You are a natural forgiver. Be careful that you do not forgive too easily or get taken advantage of. In other words, don't let your strong belief in forgiveness and emotional tendency to forgive get you into trouble.

Score 75–175: You are in the average range. You can look at your responses and decide for yourself if you want to work on becoming a more forgiving person.

Score 175–250: You have a hard time forgiving. You might want to reconsider some of your beliefs and look twice at your emotional responses. Living a life of anger and resentment is really not good for you or those around you.

Part Two

How to Forgive

# 6

# How to Forgive:
# A Practical Method

One night I went out with my wife for dinner. On the way home I suggested she take a different route. She told me that her route was the best. I told her she was stubborn. She told me I was a jerk. We didn't speak the rest of the way home. We were locked into a fight neither of us had wanted, but neither of us would back down once it got going.

When we got home, she stayed in the kitchen, while I went upstairs to bed. As I lay in bed, brooding, I thought maybe if I called downstairs and pretended nothing had happened, we would forget about the spat and make up. So, I called down and asked her if she would please bring me a little snack when she came upstairs. A few minutes later she appeared, holding up a single stalk of wilted celery—my snack. There was a pause as I took in her message. Then we both laughed. The lock of pride sprang open, and we made up.

Sometimes it happens that spontaneously, but not often. In this chapter I describe a practical method—based on research conducted by many experts, as well as my own twenty years of work as a psychiatrist—for getting past anger and resentment in those many instances when a wilted stalk of celery doesn't do the trick.

I divide the process into four stages, like acts in a play. Indeed, some of the greatest plays ever written focus on this progression of events.

Act I is **pain**: feeling wronged and wondering what to do.

Act II is **reliving what happened and reflecting on it**, using your beliefs, intelligence and imagination to help guide you. Ask yourself, *What do I want this pain to turn into?*

Act III is wrestling within yourself, or with others, as you heal, **working your way past anger and resentment** to a peaceful place.

Act IV is **taking stock and moving forward.**

Unlike the great plays we go to see, each time this play is put on, the characters change, the lines differ and the scene is new. But when forgiveness is the outcome, the general movement of emotion tends to follow the outline I described above. It is a movement from pain to growth.

The scenario has to begin with pain; why else would you need to forgive?

Almost by reflex we relive what happened. But if this is all we do, we get stuck. Growth is stunted, which is what happens in post-traumatic stress disorder, when a person has been so badly traumatized that they suffer flashbacks and can't get rid of the pain.

If you are able to reflect upon what happened as you relive it, then you can begin to take control, instead of the painful event controlling you. As you reflect you can appeal to your own personal values and philosophy as well as your intelligence to shape your future responses.

If, as you reflect, you want to rid yourself of the anger and resentment you feel, if you want to move past the pain, then you must work within yourself and work with others in a process of alchemy that turns pain into growth. This is a process, not a moment, not an event, not a deed. It takes time. It can be mysterious and unpredictable, but it will happen if you want it to. In a moment I say more about how to make it happen.

The fuel to make it happen, the motivation, derives from your answer to the question, *What do I want this pain to turn into?* If you grab yourself by your emotional collar and say, *Stop! Think!* then you will see that you do not want more pain or misery, no more recycling of the very hurt you are feeling now. You want change. You want growth.

If you allow yourself to, you will see that you want happiness now, you want peace, you want harmony. The last thing you want is more conflict, more of what you have been made to feel.

You may think it is impossible for goodness to come out of such badness, for growth and health and happiness to come out of insult, injury or even death. But they can. Many stories in this book show that it can, and millions of stories in history prove that it can. But you must resist the sweet temptation of revenge and reach for what is sweeter still.

As you work your way past the anger and resentment, you survey the new ground you have found. Your life has changed for the better, and you now are a wiser person. You have an opportunity at this point to help others in their struggles to forgive. How you do this is, of course, up to you.

Before I elaborate further, I need to emphasize that while

this approach to forgiveness is practical and learnable, it requires your improvisation and imagination to work.

Keep in mind that forgiveness remains an amorphous process. By offering this formula I do not intend to prescribe one script. You will write your own. You may switch the sequence around. You may skip parts that I mentioned and add parts of your own. You may weave in and out of the process, maybe shelving the whole enterprise for a few years, then coming back to take the next step when you are ready.

However you do it, it will be your own way, and you will follow a personal formula of your own. You will make it up as you go. You will get help where you don't expect it, and sometimes not get help where you think you should.

As I describe in more detail my own formula for forgiveness, I offer it only as the "Hallowell Formula," presented in the hope that it prompts you to synthesize your own.

# Act I:
# Pain

Forgiveness begins in pain. You get hurt by someone, some group, some company or agency, or another entity. If you are going to forgive, you first have to admit to yourself, if not to others, that you have been hurt. Some people pretend that they have not been hurt, and then they go around with a big chip on their shoulder, feeling anger without admitting it. If you have been hurt, admitting it is a good idea.

Now you start to feel a flood of emotions.

Once you admit you have been hurt, emotions trickle in, build up force and pretty soon swamp you. Depending upon how deeply you have been hurt, you may feel rage, sadness, fear, surprise, desolation, resentment, confusion, despair, murderous intentions, thoughts of suicide, or all of these and more. This flood blasts away at your emotional foundations. As the feelings pour in, they rip great holes in your sense of well-being. As you try to stay afloat in the flood, you may say and do terrible things. If you have been deeply hurt, you may well be crazy with emotion and completely out of control.

But after a while, the flood subsides. You look around and see what damage has been done inside of you and outside of you. You are thinking more rationally, but "you" are now a different person. Your world has changed. If you have been deeply hurt, it may never be the same again.

Admitting the hurt and being swept up in the flood of emotion can traumatize you deeply. You should not be alone, if you can help it. You should be with friends—in person or on the telephone. However you arrange it, you should be in contact with others.

If the hurt is minor, as in a spat with your spouse, before you try to forgive you still need to give yourself a chance to feel what you are feeling. Premature forgiveness only leads to anger later on. As unpleasant as the pain can be, you must feel it through and through before you can move on.

As you are doing this, talk to other people you trust. Connecting with others is very important, perhaps the most important step of all on the road to forgiveness.

You may also want to be alone for a while. That is good, too, but don't remain alone for too long. You can lose your sense of reality when you are isolated. It is like being in the dark. Your imagination tends to run amok. You exaggerate the negative and lose touch with the positive. In isolation, people work themselves up into fits of vengeful rage. They make bad, impulsive decisions because they read situations incorrectly.

Instead, try to find one or two people whom you trust and talk with those people about what has happened. It helps if the person you talk to has some distance on the situation and is not personally involved in it. You might talk to a therapist, a doctor, a spiritual advisor, a close relative, a friend or all of the above.

In talking to other people—and you don't need many people, just one or two or three—don't think that you have to solve anything or fix the situation. Just let yourself talk, in a confidential, unpressured atmosphere.

As you talk you will feel many conflicting emotions. A good idea is not to take action of any sort, now. You probably are entertaining fantasies of revenge. Don't act on them, at least not yet. Don't file a lawsuit, or write a letter or e-mail, or make a telephone call to the person who hurt you. Don't quit your job or leave your spouse or jump into or out of a big business deal. Give yourself some time—days, at least; probably weeks, months, even years—for your emotional system to reequilibrate.

Be sure you don't withdraw from life now; stay connected. Don't pretend that everything is okay, which is the equivalent of withdrawing. You are withdrawing from your own emotional reality.

Stay connected also to the truth of your situation. To help you do that, stay connected to your sources of positive energy. Connections to activities you like and people you love are your most important sources of healing. These connections may be to friends or to certain members of your family. The connections may also be to certain activities, like gardening or tennis perhaps. Or they may be to work, to a pet you love, to a club or other group that matters to you, or to God or your own personal philosophy or sense of the eternal. The connection may be to nature—a favorite place to walk or just to sit and watch the sky or sea. The connection may be to a piece of music that helps you reflect, or to a favorite author or a movie you love. All these kinds of what I call *connectedness* combine to help you in your life more than any other force can. Maintaining and nourishing these connections is essential as you are healing your emotional wounds.

# Act II:
# Reliving and Reflecting

After you have been hurt, you naturally relive what happened to you. As your mind fills with the painful memories, try to appeal to your beliefs and not just let your gut rule the process. Your gut will want nothing more than revenge.

This is where the active part of forgiveness matters most. Instead of passively following your gut reactions, you stop yourself and appeal to reason and to your system of beliefs. This is a key—and to my way of thinking, noble—moment, one that separates the great from the small, the heroes from the mob.

As the flood of emotions subsides, you decide what to do. Your unconscious swirls around. You may become cautious and resolve never to trust anyone again. You may resolve to take revenge. You may leave the person or group that hurt you. You may seek professional help. You may pray. Or you may resolve never to pray again.

Somewhere in here it helps if you deliberately appeal to your values in life. Ask yourself the question I have suggested before: *What do I want this pain to turn into?* Based upon who you are and what has happened to you in life up until now, you have a system of ideals. Turn to them and let them guide you, if you can. Otherwise, the basest parts of you will take over.

Maybe what has been done to you has shaken your values so badly that they are broken and are of no use to you anymore. Maybe you now look at values like love or forgiveness as silly or even dangerous. Maybe you now look at such values as the very reason that you were hurt in the first place. Maybe you have become a cynic or a justifiably angry, bitter person.

Maybe now your new values tell you to take revenge. Maybe your values tell you that once you have been attacked, you should not rest until you have attacked back and attacked harder. Maybe you are ready to kill.

On the other hand, maybe in the rubble of the flood, other values survive. Maybe you look over and see the pillar of forgiveness still standing, and maybe you go over and lean against it for support.

In this crucial period of looking at the damage and deciding what to do, it is crucial, if you can, to use as your guide what you value most. Primitive parts of you will urge you toward anger and revenge. If those are what you believe in and value most, then go to them. But if not, resist them. Your more advanced beliefs—formed long before the wrong was ever done and long before the emotional flood—are what can hold you now and keep you from committing yourself to hatred.

If you believe in forgiveness—and I have tried to make a case for it in previous chapters—now is the time to act on that belief. Your gut is clamoring for revenge, so now is time for you to choose. Don't be passive. While will alone can't produce forgiveness, it is all but impossible to forgive against your will.

It also helps if wise others counsel you now. Don't listen to the mob. It helps if you have friends, a spouse, a physician or clergy, or an advisor who can help you search within yourself for what your true beliefs are. Not for what feels good— that would most likely be revenge—but for what you believe in, for what you'd hope your children would do.

If your beliefs lead you to want to forgive, you are on the route to forgiveness. But you are not there yet.

You must also grieve what was lost. Try to acknowledge the sadness you are feeling. Instead of letting anger take over, try to look beneath the anger and feel the sadness. You are sad because something did not work the way you wanted. You have lost something, like hope or trust in someone, or the chance to do something you wanted. Grieving means letting yourself feel your sadness fully and completely. This takes time and patience.

As I mentioned before, forgiveness represents your letting go of your hope that the past will be different. You need to accept that what happened actually did happen, and that it cannot unhappen. You can't change it, no matter how much anger you muster or revenge you exact. So, now you should feel the sadness, know the pain, grieve your loss and move on, leaving anger and resentment behind.

If the matter is a minor one, like a spat with your spouse, this "grieving" process will be trivial and brief. But better to allow yourself to feel a bit sad than to rush off into anger, where you will only make matters worse.

After you grieve, or while you are grieving, think. Look for what I call the hook. After you have grieved, in all likelihood you still will not have reached forgiveness. You will still be stuck in resentment, hooked by anger. Now, you must look for the hook that has you hooked! I develop this idea more in a later chapter, but the basic point is this: When you can't reach forgiveness, even though you want to, it is usually because anger and resentment have hooked you and hold you back in ways you can't see. You can't free yourself, even though you want to. So you have to find the hook. You can do this by asking yourself, *Why does this offense bother me so much? What is holding me back?*

Your answer to this question will vary depending upon who you are and what has happened to you in life up until now. The question therefore takes into account your own personal story, your own individual psychology. Maybe you have a hot spot when it comes to issues of control, and that's what's hooking you. Or maybe you unconsciously always feel people are taking advantage of you, and that's what's hooking you. Or maybe you project feelings toward your father and mother onto others when you feel hurt, and that's what's hooking you.

You are your own person, individual and complex in your own way. I can't tell you in advance what is hooking you; to do so would be facile and simple-minded of me. This step is where you must look into your own self and consider what is going on.

Again, the question to ask yourself, the question that should guide you to the hook, is this: *Why does this offense bother me so much?*

To help yourself in looking for the hook, try asking yourself this very difficult question: *Might I be acting like a fool?* My uncle and father lost a close friendship between brothers out of foolish pride. I am sure you know someone who has done the same, yet it is awfully difficult to tell people they are acting like fools. What a blessing if you can tell yourself! You are probably the one person who can do it. So, take a moment. Let your anger subside, if you can. Then ask yourself, *In what way might I be acting like a fool here? Is this grudge really worth it?*

Along the way, do what you need to do to regain your feelings of control and safety. Often we keep raging inside, not because we are angry as much as we are afraid. We are afraid that we will get hurt again. We are afraid that only by being angry can we be safe. We use anger to ward off the other person, to bolster our own sense of power and to give us a feeling of control. So, if you find yourself unable to let go of your anger and resentment, you might need to take steps to make yourself feel safer. Anger and resentment may be like alarm signals telling you it is not yet safe to forgive.

What you need to do to feel safe depends, of course, upon your particular situation. You may need extreme measures, such as getting a restraining order or seeing that someone goes to jail, before you feel safe enough to forgive. But usually what you need will be less extreme. You may need to get validation from others that what happened was wrong. You may need to get an apology. You may need to be reminded that you are more powerful than you feel that you are. You may need to be reminded that the other person is not as powerful as you imagine he or she is.

In any case, don't force forgiveness if you feel afraid. Instead, listen to your fear and do what you must to regain your feeling of safety.

Also, try to empathize with the person or people who hurt you. One of the best prods to forgiveness is putting yourself in the shoes of the one(s) who hurt you. Hard to do! But try to see the situation from their point of view. I know, I know, that seems impossible. But given time, you probably can find your way to putting yourself in the other person's shoes, even if you detest those shoes. If you can't empathize, you have lost something valuable within yourself.

The Dalai Lama tells the story of a Tibetan monk who had served eighteen brutal months in a Chinese prison. After the monk's release the Dalai Lama asked the monk what his biggest fear had been while he was imprisoned. He answered that his greatest fear was losing his compassion for the Chinese, his tormentors. To lose that would be to lose what he prized most.

Few of us are like that Tibetan monk or anywhere near the Dalai Lama in our compassion for our fellow humans. But we can still feel compassion for our enemies, if we remind ourselves that compassion protects *us*. The Tibetan monk feared losing his compassion for his enemies, not because he was such a goody-goody saintly guy, but because if he lost that he knew he would become vulnerable to the ravages of hatred. He knew—and we should know—that compassion protected him against hatred, and hatred is a poison that kills the best parts of us.

The old saying, "To understand all is to forgive all," points up the healing power of empathy. Sometimes you simply cannot empathize, which is all right. But at least try. Empathy is a crucial tool in the toolbox of forgiveness. It opens the door to love—even for your enemies.

# Act III:
# Working It Out

Now wrestle within yourself to flatten the hook.

Maybe the hook is some form of foolishness, like jealousy, pride or stubbornness. If so, and you see the fool in you, then you can flatten the hook merely by consciously overruling your crazed emotions. Time helps, but effort speeds the process.

If you flatten the hook, then you can spit it out. There are many hooks, and you can flatten them in many ways. Your empathy for the person who hurt you may already have helped flatten the hook. Here are some other methods:

## Think; Use Insight

Just think about it. Most of the time, anger and resentment hurt you more than the person you are targeting. This is a useful insight, one that we always overlook when we carry grudges, fuming for years on end about how we have been wronged. Like fuming after you hit a bad golf shot, ongoing rage makes your game worse. You will be far better off if you expel the toxins of anger and resentment. Just that insight alone might be enough to flatten the hook, given time.

## Pray or Meditate

Depending upon your spiritual predilection, you may turn to prayer or meditation to help you flatten the hook. Almost all prayerful practices and modes of meditation help people spit out the hooks of spite, rage, resentment and revenge. As you pray for help, or as you meditate upon serene emptiness, you may begin to feel the barbs gradually go limp inside you.

## Give Thanks

Try to regain perspective by giving thanks for what is good in your life. As you allow yourself to visualize the good in your life, and feel the positive energy that emanates from it, you will find the hook much more apt to slip out. Recognizing the positive lubricates the way for the negative to slide away.

## Imagine Vengeance

Odd advice in a book on forgiveness? Maybe, but sometimes images of vengeance can help. A few daydreams of revenge can actually make you feel better, as if you had taken revenge without actually doing any harm. Just don't fall into the trap of becoming hooked on the fantasies of revenge; they can be a dangerous drug.

### Focus on the Future

Another way to flatten the hook was put succinctly by the seventeenth-century poet George Herbert, who said, "Living well is the best revenge." Focus on living well. As you enjoy your life, you find the hook flattens on its own.

### Remind Yourself That You and the World Will Be Better Off If You Forgive

This is like walking away from the bar after you've had enough to drink. After you have tasted some sweet, imagined revenge, walk away—before you get drunk on it and maybe ruin your life.

### Remind Yourself That You Need Forgiveness, Too

This bit of insight helps change your frame of mind. The best way to puncture self-righteousness is to be reminded of how unrighteous we all are. "Let him who is without sin cast the first stone" is how Jesus made this point. However you make it to yourself, make it and believe it. Acknowledging your own need to be forgiven is an excellent way to open your heart to forgive others.

# Act IV:
# Taking Stock and Moving Forward

Now try to renounce your anger and resentment. You are far enough along in this process to start to give it a try. Anger and resentment may reappear, like trolls and gnomes, but you should repeatedly banish them, saying, "Go away, you ugly things, I don't want you, I don't need you, you mess me up, so go away." As the trolls reappear, you continue to renounce them, sending them off. You will probably never be totally free of them, but you can certainly keep them from taking permanent residence in your heart.

Repeat what you have done until the anger stays gone.

Once the hook is flattened and gone, and the anger and resentment have been renounced, you have still not completed the process. The hook of anger and resentment has a way of reemerging inside you even after you think you've pulled it out. So, you have to flatten it once again, by whatever means works best for you, and pull it out all over again. You might have to do this a dozen times, or a dozen dozen or more. If you keep at it, sooner or later the hook will stay gone, and you will be free. You will have reached forgiveness at last.

Be nourished by this act of forgiveness and grow from it. Taste and digest the delicious fruit of forgiveness. It makes you grow healthy, happy and strong. After you have managed to forgive, *enjoy what you have done.* You have made yourself into a better person. You have contributed something positive to the world around you. You have created a fresh, clean space within you and outside of you as well. Where there had been anger and resentment, with fantasies of revenge, tension and turmoil, now there is clear air. You are healthier. You are happier. You have grown spiritually, and it is good to relish this growth. Enjoy it. Tell others about it. Let others know that it is possible. Celebrate forgiveness as a practical and realistic strategy in life.

Help others in their efforts to forgive. If you can tell others about your efforts to forgive, that will help them do likewise.

A lot of the work of forgiveness is simply overcoming cynicism or disappointed hopes. Hearing from someone else that they were able to do it, and how much better it made them feel, helps you do it yourself.

❊   ❊   ❊

Here is a summary of the whole play, act by act, scene by scene, as I have written it:

## Act I: Pain and Hurt
### Scene:

1. You suffer some kind of hurt.

Then you:

2. Live through the flood of emotion. This takes time.
3. Talk to other people you trust.
4. Don't withdraw from life. Stay connected.

## Act II: Reliving and Reflecting
### Scene:

5. Appeal to your beliefs. Ask, *What do I want my pain to turn into?*
6. Grieve the loss of whatever this wrong robbed you of.
7. Look for the hook that makes you unable to forgive.
8. Consider how you might possibly be acting like a fool.
9. Do what you need to do to regain your feeling of safety and control.
10. Empathize with the person or people who hurt you.

## Act III: Working It Out
### Scene:

11. Wrestle within yourself to flatten the hook.
12. Think; use insight.
13. Pray or meditate upon the situation.
14. Give thanks for what you have.
15. Imagine vengeance.
16. Focus on the future.
17. Remind yourself that you and the world will be better off if you forgive.
18. Remind yourself that you need forgiveness, too.

## Act IV: Taking Stock and Moving Forward
### Scene:

19. Renounce your anger and resentment.
20. Repeat these steps as often as you need to until the hook stays out and the anger is gone.
21. Be nourished by this act of forgiveness and grow from it.
22. Help others in their efforts to forgive.

# How This Process Can Work in Real Life

Let me give you two examples of forgiveness. One example is of a man who suffered a very major wrong as a child and who managed to forgive as an adult. The other example is of a trivial, everyday offense, the kind of issue most of us must often deal with.

I'll start with the trivial example, which I will take from my own life. It is a common occurrence—getting cut off in traffic—that most people can identify with, and which will allow me to demonstrate the process, step by step, in an uncomplicated way.

So, there I am one day, driving along in Boston, and, as happens every day, some big, old gas-guzzler, like a beat-up Cadillac, careens from one lane to the next, forcing me to jam on my brakes to avoid a collision. When I honk, the clueless driver flips me his middle finger and speeds on, spewing fumes as he goes.

I am left hurt, enraged, humiliated, at odds with life. At that moment, I hate not only the man who cut me off, but the human condition to boot. Emotion has flooded me. Fortunately, I preserve control well enough to keep driving. I say to myself, *Let it go,* but the rage continues inside.

I wouldn't ordinarily proceed through the process of forgiveness scene by scene or step by step, in an organized fashion, but for the sake of demonstration, let's say I did. We've already seen steps 1 and 2. Step 3 is impossible, as I am alone in the car. I can remember conversations with trusted others, however, conversations in which we agreed that road rage was real and dangerous and not a good thing to give in to. Step 4, not withdrawing from life, is also not applicable to me in the car. Step 5, however, is. When I said, *Let it go,* I was essentially appealing to my beliefs.

If I had asked, *What do I want this pain to turn into?* it would have been clear to me that I did not want it to turn into a traffic accident, a fistfight, my going to jail, or either the bad driver or me getting killed. That would be very stupid, not to mention sad.

Then I come to step 6: Grieve the loss. What had I lost? A

bit of pride. A bit of faith in humanity. A bit of adrenaline, which was spent in the startled reaction the crazy driver set off in me. *Isn't it sad,* I would say to myself, *that the world isn't a perfect place?* Gradually, I could let myself feel sad, rather than mad.

But the anger might persist. Step 7. Find the hook. Why do such drivers bother me sooooo much? My wife can forget them in a second. I brood. Why? Because I am a primitive, proud male. Because, like most males, I turn traffic into a competition, and that driver had just won. He had *cut me off,* and how Freudian do you have to be to see the symbolism in *that?*

Okay. So the hook in this instance is my foolish, male, macho pride. On to step 8. How might I be acting like a fool? By giving in to my foolish, male, macho pride. Now is the time to use insight, and then use willpower to stop acting like a fool. I still felt a bit of the rage, but I told myself it was stupid and to cut it out.

As for step 9, regaining safety and control, this was important. I had to remind myself that the crazy driver in the beat-up Cadillac was *not* a realistic threat to my manhood. He was only as much of a threat as my imagination turned him into. It was my own sense of vulnerability that made him feel so powerful to me. In fact, I was safe. I was in control. We men need to remind ourselves of this . . . *often.*

Step 10. Empathize with the person who hurt me. Well, now that I had defanged him, I could see him as some fun-loving guy who was just foolin' around . . . or something. I have to admit, I didn't have much empathy for him, until I remembered that in my younger days *I had done exactly the same kind of thing.* Okay. Empathy.

Step 11. Wrestle within to flatten the hook. By now it was pretty flat. I didn't have to wrestle all that much, once I saw myself in the guy in the Cadillac.

Step 12. Insight. I had already done this.

Step 13. Prayer or meditation? Not needed, but sometimes I do pray for patience in traffic.

Step 14. Give thanks for what you have. I actually do that when I resist anger in traffic. Once I quiet down inside I think of my wife and our three kids, and I feel grateful that I did not do anything to jeopardize them.

Step 15. Imagine vengeance. I had done that much earlier.

Step 16. Focus on the future. Yes, it was time to keep my eye on the road and think about better things.

Step 17. Yes, I was better off having forgiven the crazy driver, and the world was better off, too. We avoided a big accident.

Step 18. Remind myself that I need forgiveness, too. I had already done that, when it dawned on me that I had been as big of a jerk in my own life as that driver had been to me.

Step 19. Renounce my anger and resentment. It was pretty well gone by now. I felt better without it. I didn't need Step 20, a repetition of the steps.

Step 21. Be nourished by this act of forgiveness and grow from it. Too bad that I couldn't be so nourished that I'd never need to go through this again!

Step 22. Help others. Well, I am writing this book. I hope it helps!

That is a quick and lighthearted outline of the process. Let me offer a more serious example, one in which all the steps were not specifically followed, but many were.

This story is of a man who was sexually abused by a priest in Massachusetts. It all came out during the very public period in the late 1990s and early 2000s when a sexual abuse scandal in the Catholic Church rocked the nation, especially Massachusetts, leading to the resignation of Cardinal Bernard Law.

I had known the man whose story I cite here—let me call him Tom—for years. I was shocked when he said to me one day, "Did you see the account of Father Porter on the news?" Of course I had. Everyone had. "Well, I was one of the boys he molested," he said.

Some time later, when I told him I was writing this book, Tom offered to sit down with me and tell me the story of how he had managed to forgive Father Porter. Although he did not explicitly follow the steps of the method I outlined in this chapter, as I tell his story and quote his words, you will see some of the steps covered in how he reached a place of forgiveness. (I have not changed the name of the priest here, as his correct name is part of public record.) "At the age of eleven," Tom told me,

I was an altar boy in North Attleboro, at St. Mary's Church. I saw this as a great honor, a great privilege. I had to learn all kinds of Latin phrases and all sorts of intricate procedures. It was a big deal. The priest in charge was Father Porter. He played baseball with the kids and sang "Happy Birthday" on our birthdays. He was the guy everyone wanted to be like.

That's when the abuse happened to me. Father Porter would have get-togethers with us kids. And he'd abuse kids right in front of us. You just suspended your belief that something wrong was going on. He would fondle me, and I wouldn't put up a fight. I was lost. I didn't know what to say. You couldn't tell him he was wrong because *he* was the guy who decided what was right or wrong. This went on for a couple of years. He molested many boys. Then, one day, he got reassigned.

I forgot all about it. But when I was forty years old, the story appeared on the news on TV, and suddenly it all came back to me in vivid detail. That was the start of my dealing with it. I just tried to talk about it as much as I could. I talked about it publicly, I talked about it with the others it had happened to, the other survivors.

Tom told me the key to his getting past anger and resentment was talking to others and not withdrawing. He set in motion a process that eventually led him to forgiveness.

It was also clear in talking to Tom how glad he was that this terrible pain had, in fact, turned into something positive for him. He was sad that the same result had not taken place for so many others.

The whole process of taking control and being public about it was very important. I didn't have to be secret anymore and protect the person who had done this. It was so hard to label as bad the person whose essence was supposed to be good. Gradually, I came to terms with it and saw him as flawed, but all of us are flawed. I had to remember that. Maybe he was more deeply flawed, but the jagged edges and crazy-making contradictions came off as I talked about it all.

Also, the experience of talking to the other survivors was amazing. I was one of the few who had survived intact. It helped me a lot to be of help to them.

I really think in order to forgive someone you need to regain your own feeling of control. I don't know that anyone earns forgiveness. The person who is forgiven can't really control that.

But also, in order to forgive, you have to somehow empathize. I have forgiven Father Porter. I don't feel anger and resentment. I see him as a sick person. He did come up for parole, and I didn't think he should be paroled, as he has not come to terms with what he did and who he is.

In court I just felt pity for him. That's amazing, because all those years ago I thought he was the savior, this incredibly charismatic guy. That day in court I realized he didn't have any of the power I thought he held over us. He was disarmed. There wasn't any need to hate him, because I was no longer afraid of him.

To sum it up for me, if you can regain your sense of control, you can forgive.

You can see in Tom's story many of the steps I suggest. But Tom did not follow any outline; he followed his heart. I simply offer the outline for those times when your heart gets stuck and you don't know what to do.

※　※　※

Obviously, the process I outline in this chapter is not fool-proof. I can't stand up and hawk my "forgiveness method" with such slogans as, "Feel guilty? Just read this!" Or, "Want to forgive or be forgiven? Just follow these simply, easy steps!" If anyone truly came up with a surefire, foolproof method of forgiveness, it would be front-page, Nobel Peace Prize–winning news. World conflict would end. Lawsuits would disappear. Divorce rates would plummet. Death rates would fall. We would all live longer and happier lives.

So let me apologize for presuming to offer "a practical approach" to forgiveness. I don't mean to make the process sound prefabricated, as if you could buy it off the shelf at Home Depot. Forgiveness is so often mysterious, unexpected and far beyond the practical planning of any human mind that a formula for doing it can seem absurd or at best simplis-tic. I understand forgiveness well enough to know that it escapes capture by any formula and that it often originates in parts of us that we don't understand, can't see and certainly can't control.

Some chance event, some happy coincidence, some odd moment that we never planned can be what sparks forgive-ness, like my wife Sue appearing with the wilted stalk of cel-ery. Neither of us planned the impact of that moment. Indeed, Sue picked up the stalk of celery with spitefulness in her heart. But it just so happened that the celery made us both laugh, and so we made up. Any "formula" for forgive-ness must begin simply by urging us all to be open to the unexpected impulse to make up, whether sparked by a stalk of celery, a sneeze or some other moment that changes how we feel.

You don't know how or when such a moment will happen. You simply need to be open to it, as open as Robert Frost was when he was walking through the woods one day and felt some snow fall down on him from the branch of a tree. Later he wrote this poem to describe how that moment changed his day:

> *The way a crow*
> *Shook down on me*
> *The dust of snow*
> *From a hemlock tree*
> *Has given my heart*
> *A change of mood*
> *And saved some part*
> *Of a day I had rued.*

Snow is traditionally pure and white; hemlock traditionally evil. But snow can fall from a hemlock tree; good can come from evil. So it is with forgiveness. It can unexpectedly fall down upon us, even from evil branches, like the dust of snow from a hemlock tree.

But when it does not sprinkle down spontaneously, when you must reach higher and farther than your grasp allows to try to shake it down, then forgiveness requires patience. The word "patience" means the power of suffering, being able to suffer without striking back. Being hurt usually makes people want to hurt those who hurt them, so forgiveness must get in the way of this rampaging, virulent human desire. Getting in the way of it is treacherous, if not futile. You have to be brave, and you have to be convinced that forgiving is the right thing to do. Then you can try to reach into the darkness of your imagination and grope around until you find the white hot coal of hurt and hatred, which you must grab onto long enough to pull it out before its heat makes you drop it and leave it inside.

So how can you do such a difficult deed? You can find your own ways, as most of us do, or you might try the method I have offered here, a method that might just help you hold onto that coal of anger long enough to get it out.

But I also know that the very idea of forgiveness trembles in the sight of certain crimes. Simon Wiesenthal, in his book *The Sunflower,* tells an amazing story from when he was imprisoned in a Nazi concentration camp. Through a long series of events he details in the book, one day he found himself being asked for forgiveness by a member of the SS who was dying. This man had been directly responsible for the torture and execution of men, women and children Wiesenthal knew, all innocent victims who died at this man's hands. How could Wiesenthal forgive such a man, no matter how sincere his request or how deep his repentance? Unable to respond, Wiesenthal did not reply to the SS officer's plea for forgiveness. He remained silent.

I have no idea what I would have done. Do you?

Because of stories like that, I cannot tell anyone that they should forgive. All I know, as a doctor, is that people are better off if they do—somehow—forgive.

*The student goes to the Master and says, "Master, I have been meditating long and hard, but I cannot forgive mankind."*

*"What is it you are trying to forgive mankind for having done?" the Master asks.*

*"All the evil people do," the student replies.*

*The Master hits the student with a stick.*

*The student falls to the ground and stands up rubbing his head. "Master, why did you hit me?" he asks.*

*The Master hits the student again, even harder.*

*Once again the student falls to the ground. This time as he stands up he has blood dripping down his face. "Master, why did you hit me again?" the student asks.*

*The Master hits the student a third time, harder still.*

*The student collapses. He remains crumpled at the Master's feet. "Why are you beating me?" he asks, his hands covering his head.*

*"You tell me," the Master replies, then walks away.*

*The student goes home and meditates and studies for weeks and months, but no answer comes to him.*

*Summoning up his courage, the student returns to the Master, this time keeping a bit of a distance. "Master, I have been trying to discern why you beat me, but I cannot find an answer."*

*The Master replies, "But I see that you are keeping a distance from me now."*

*"Yes," the student replies, "because I fear that you will hit me again."*

*"You have devised a strategy," the Master observes.*

*"Yes," the student admits. "But that is all."*

*"You still wonder why I beat you," the Master states.*

*"Yes," the student responds, "I do."*

*"Because I like to beat you," the Master replies. "Why else would I do it?"*

*"But why do you like to beat me?" the student asks.*

*"Because it's fun!" the Master replies with delight.*

*"But why is it fun to see me suffer?" the student asks.*

*"It is the way humans are made," the Master replies and walks away.*

*The student goes home and meditates and studies for months. But he cannot discern why his Master should find it fun to see him suffer, nor does he believe that it is the way we humans are made. So he returns to the Master.*

*"Master, I have studied and meditated for months, but I have not been able to discern why a wise and kind teacher like you should find it fun to watch me suffer."*

*"Come closer," the Master says.*

*"If I come closer, will you hit me again?" the student asks.*

*"What do you think?" the Master replies.*

*"I fear that you will, but I hope that you won't," answers the student.*

*"And if I do, will you forgive me?" the Master asks.*

*"What do you mean by 'forgive'?" the student asks.*

*"I mean, will you let me hit you again?"*

*At that, the student wonders if he should find a new Master.*

*The Master senses what his student is thinking. "You may look for a new Master. I am sure you can find many. But sooner or later, you will find yourself at this point once again."*

*"But what am I to do?" the student protests. "Is the purpose of all my studying to teach me that my teachers like to beat me?"*

*"You look to me for answers, and all I give you is beatings," the Master replies. "When you ask me why, I tell you beating you gives me pleasure. You have trusted me, studied hard, given up years of your life believing that I was leading you to a more enlightened place. And yet here you are."*

*"I don't understand," the student says sadly.*

*The teacher sighs. "It is not that you don't understand, but that you won't understand. People like to hurt people. This feeling lives in you, too."*

*The student falls silent. Then he speaks, with anger in his voice. "Master, either you have a false heart and are an evil person in disguise, or you are trying to teach me that my studying is foolish and that life itself is evil." At that, the student draws closer, close enough to be hit. "If either is true, you might as well hit me again," he says.*

*The Master smiles and breaks his stick in half over his knee. "Now you are starting to learn about forgiveness," he replies.*

# 7

# Everyday Forgiveness

I hope I have not sounded as if I think forgiveness is easy. It can be extraordinarily difficult, even in ordinary situations. Let me give you some ordinary examples from my own life.

Not long ago, my wife Sue and I took our three young children and five of their small friends to Six Flags Over New England, an amusement park that is about a two-hour drive from where we live in Arlington, Massachusetts. The trip was harrowing. Organizing and keeping track of eight children in a crowded amusement park is like keeping track of mice in a warehouse.

As the final hour of the eight hours we spent at the park ticked its way to its end, I was hot and tired and I craved a cold drink. I found a drink stand and stood in the drink line, trying to be patient and composed, as a grown man is supposed to be. But when a young woman cut directly in front of me, put her money down and took a Mountain Dew, I spoke up and proclaimed the all-too-obvious, "Hey, you just cut in line!"

The young woman smiled at me sarcastically and said, "Get over it," then walked away, tossing back her head to guzzle her Mountain Dew proudly, defiantly—evilly, if you'd asked me at the time.

I fixed my eyes on her as she walked away and imagined all the injustice in the world concentrated within this one young woman, an alien who needed to be destroyed. My lips curled as I hurled an insult at her about how entitled she was. This retort was as lost on her as if I had stated it in Chinese. As much as I despised her for what she had done, I despised her even more for making me feel so ineffectual. I couldn't even insult the woman with words that would penetrate her sneer. That, in turn, made me even more angry. Now my hatred was amplified by humiliation and shame. Not only had she cut in front of me, she had taunted me and gotten away with it. I could do nothing but hate her.

My kids weren't looking—they were with Sue—so I could have let rip with some really bad words, if I wanted to. I could even have gone after the woman and demanded that she apologize. I could have slapped her or beaten her up. Or, more in keeping with who I am, I could have interrogated her on the system of morality she subscribed to, and pointed out to her that it was behavior like hers that had always ruined the world and was still ruining it to this day. I could have composed an entire speech and forced her to listen, along with the crowd that would have quickly gathered around. Thank God, I did none of those things.

But I did imagine doing them. I stood there, seething, drinking the cold drink I had at last procured, entertaining scenes of vengeance against this young woman, until, gradually, my temperature cooled down and my reason was restored. But, for a few seconds, maybe half a minute, I had been in a dangerously furious state, my mind swimming with rage and shame and hatred. I was in the state of mind in which ordinary people do extraordinarily bad deeds. Shame is the hidden ingredient that, when added to anger, makes it so dangerous. Unfortunately, moments of anger combined with shame abound in daily life, which makes it amazing not that we sometimes kill each other, but that we don't kill each other much more frequently.

If a woman at an amusement park could lead me to lick my lips at the thought of violent confrontation and retribution, or if the person who cut me off in traffic the day before could do the same thing, then isn't it amazing that I never have actually killed anyone, or even assaulted someone?

Actually, to tell the truth, I once did commit an assault. I assaulted a car. I was living in New Orleans as a medical student at Tulane. One evening I was looking for a parking space in the French Quarter, a section of the city notoriously low on on-street parking. Just as I found a prized empty space and started to back into it, a small-sized BMW zipped in headfirst and stole my spot.

My judgment snapped. Before I could think of what I was doing, I stopped my car and stormed out of it, slamming the car door so hard I'm surprised something didn't break. I could see the young man and woman in the BMW hurriedly rolling up their windows and locking their doors as they saw this lunatic—me—bearing down upon them. I didn't want to break their windows; I just couldn't stand letting them steal my spot without some act of revenge.

Suddenly, the driver of that BMW represented evil, just as the woman had done who cut in line at Six Flags. The driver of the BMW radiated evil and symbolized all the people who had ever taken advantage not only of me but of people in general, especially people, like me, who never could afford a BMW. At that moment, on behalf of all of us, like Mel Gibson in *Braveheart,* I had to act.

What I did was guided by forces beyond my control. I truly do not remember deciding to do what I did next. I just did it, as if it had been preprogrammed into my genetic code thousands of years before I was born, which, indeed, it probably was.

I walked over to the car, climbed up onto the hood like an ape, pounded the windshield with my fists, then climbed up onto the roof. From my perch atop the BMW I let my legs dangle over the side and started kicking the driver's closed window with the leather heels of my shoes. I didn't break the window, but I guess I led the guy to believe I was crazy enough to do real damage.

In moments, he rolled down his window and said, "Okay, okay, I'll let you have the parking spot. Just stop kicking my car."

Sliding forward, I jumped down onto the pavement and proudly supervised this man's exodus from my promised land. Saving his pride, he flipped me off as he drove away, but I had won the battle, or so I thought at the time.

Was it worth it that I risked my life, not to mention the lives of the people in the car, over that parking spot? Of course not. Today, I thank God that I wasn't killed that night, or on the many other days and nights when I have acted brazenly out of anger.

There is a primitive part of me—and of most of us,

especially us men—that rises up out of the depths when crossed, challenged or demeaned. My life and the lives of others depend upon my ability to control that part of me.

One good way to gain control is to train myself out of the habit of vengeance. One good way to learn how to do that is not to take all insults personally. The more you can see what a person does as being governed by conflicts within that person, having nothing to do with you personally, the less inclined you will be toward vengeance.

I have made some progress in this regard. You will notice that I did not do the equivalent of getting onto the roof of the car of the young woman who cut in front of me in the line for cold drinks. I *imagined* doing it, but I didn't actually do it. That progress is probably all that I will make in this lifetime. I didn't look at the woman who cut in front of me and imagine the conflicts in her life that might have led her to become such an obnoxious, entitled person. In theory I know it would have helped me calm down, but I am not quite there yet in practice. I doubt I will ever remove from my mind its tendency to imagine revenge. But if I can keep from recklessly trying to take revenge, as I did that muggy night in New Orleans, then I will have made great progress.

That is not to say there is no outlet for anger when you have been wronged. Living well—turning that anger into constructive activity—really is the healthiest way to "get even."

About twenty years ago, when I was just finishing my training in psychiatry, I was trying to decide how to ply my trade, now that all my years of preparation were coming to a close. What I really wanted to do was teach part-time, see patients part-time and write books part-time, but a doctor who ran a hospital was recruiting me to come work for him full-time. He was offering me a lot of money, and as I had debts but no savings, a lot of money was tempting. But I didn't like this guy. Profit was his only motivation; if I took the job he was offering me, I would be selling out, rather than doing what I loved. I'll never forget what that doctor said to me in our final conversation, when I declined his offer.

"You're making a very big mistake," he said in his usual, confident voice. "I am offering you a great opportunity, much better than you'll find anywhere else. Instead, you're telling me you want to be just another shrink who wants to write books that no one will read. Go ahead. Give it a try. Then come back and see me in a few years. Who knows, maybe I'll still be willing to hire you."

That was twenty years ago. I followed my bliss, as Joseph Campbell would say. I never went back to speak to that doctor, but I have thought of him often. He did me a great favor, insulting me as he did. He increased my motivation to do what I loved. And living well really is the best revenge.

But in families, living well doesn't seem to help. Only revenge will do, or so it often seems.

"I hate you!" I growled at my cousin, "and I will never, ever, ever forgive you." I was fifteen years old, and at that moment I meant what I said with every nerve in my body. My cousin, Josselyn, had betrayed a confidence, leaving me humiliated and full of rage. She had teased me in front of a couple of my friends about a girl I had a crush on. She thought I stood no chance with that girl, and she let me know it in the most taunting of terms. Within a few hours my rage had subsided, but my resolve not to forgive her had hardened into bone. She had committed an offense for which there was no forgiveness, as far as I was concerned.

I started living my life as if my cousin didn't exist. As we were like brother and sister, and lived next to each other, this was a big deal. I didn't speak to her, I didn't make eye contact with her, I didn't acknowledge her invitation to talk about what had happened. I was punishing her in the best way I knew how—by denying her existence.

That she was my closest relative in the world—my confidante, advisor, friend, supporter and soul mate—didn't matter. I was the injured party. She had committed the crime. She would have to pay. I would shun her forever.

I went through my days ignoring her. I saw my other friends, I saw her brother, I went to the movies and did what I usually did: talked about my plans and my life with other people. I told the stories I would usually have told her to other people instead, and I pretended that they understood and "got it" as perfectly as she always did—knowing, of course, that they didn't. But I was resolute; I shut her out completely.

Every time I would think about calling her up, I would say to myself, *No, you must stand your ground. There is a principle involved here. You can't let her betray you and get away with it. Who does she think she is, gossiping like that, playing with your feelings? Who needs her anyway?* I dug in, like a man of principle.

I was miserable.

I don't remember now how I made up with her. All I know is that we reconciled, then resumed our very close relationship.

What was really going on back then? My cousin had hurt my feelings, wounded my pride, betrayed my confidence and left me feeling foolish in the eyes of other people. I felt that the only way I could restore my self-respect was to hurt the person who had hurt me.

So, I set up my embargo. I did not let any communication pass from me to her. I withdrew my attention, in the hope of making her feel as bad as she had made me feel.

That's where the toxins of vengeance start: in feeling bad. It only takes a second or two of feeling really bad—humiliated, gypped, overlooked, insulted, mistreated—to set off a lifelong feud. Once the positions are set, the feelings may wax and wane, but the two parties may never reconcile.

The moment Josselyn did what she did, taunting me like that in front of friends, I hated her intensely and I told her so. I had no intention whatsoever of forgiving her, ever. When I made my grand statement, "I hate you, and I will never, ever, ever forgive you," I had set my position with such vehemence that I felt I could never, ever change it. Pride cemented it in place.

My intense feeling gradually subsided as the neurotransmitters and stress hormones dissipated. The fact is, a person cannot physically stay enraged for very long. Your body chemistry can't support that intensity of emotion indefinitely. Just as you can't remain in a state of intense anxiety or panic for very long, you can't remain irate much more than fifteen minutes. You can take a break and get irate again, but you have to take a break, for purely physical reasons if for no other. Your body has to resynthesize its chemicals of rage, much like a shooter having to reload his weapon.

During this period of "reloading," I regained conscious control of myself. Most violent crimes and murders occur during the flash of rage; if you can control yourself through that, you will probably not do anything disastrous.

Now, under conscious control, I used my time to plot my revenge. No longer frothing at the mouth (I don't know if I actually frothed, but I might just as well have, given how mad I was), I could play the chess game we all have played, trying to make someone who has hurt us feel as bad—or worse—as they made us feel.

My plan was the oldest one in the book: the silent treatment. The ancients used to punish traitors by exiling them. It was considered a punishment worse than death. Many religious sects to this day punish transgressors by commanding members of the community to shun the person. We so need the contact of others that when it is withdrawn totally we suffer deeply. If it goes on too long we get sick and die.

Of course, I couldn't exile Josselyn or command the whole town to shun her; I could only shun her myself, which I set to doing with a vengeance, quite literally.

What happened next is what so often happens. *I* suffered. She suffered a bit as well, but not nearly as much as I did. In my attempt to *show her,* I only showed myself how much I missed her when she wasn't in my life.

But now I had pride holding me back. How could I go to her and make up? *She* was supposed to come to *me.* If I went to her, I would compound my humiliation, or so I imagined. She had approached me once, and I had rejected her offer. Now my only face-saving strategy was to hope she eventually would approach me again, and maybe even again after that, depending on if the second approach seemed sincere enough.

Stubborn pride. Being male. Not knowing or wanting to

know reliable methods that facilitate forgiveness. These are some of the obstacles I faced once I uttered those words, "I hate you and I'll never, ever, ever forgive you."

I don't remember how I ever moved past those obstacles. I imagine Josselyn orchestrated the reconciliation. That would have been like her. It was her way to stir the pot, then it was her way to settle it down. She probably made some joke I couldn't laugh at, then she probably said something like, "Oh, let's be friends again, I miss you," and I probably forgot all about the "principle" I was standing on. As I said, I am pretty sure Josselyn helped me, as that was the way it usually was. She made sure people got back together.

But what if you're not someone who makes sure of that? You can maintain a feud, based more on pride than on principle, for the rest of your life—unless you find a way out. Unless you find a way past pride, past shunning, past exile, back to connection.

The ways are not hard to find, really. How hard is it to do what I imagine Josselyn did, and knock gently on the door? And how hard is it to do what I must have done, and respond?

All we had to do was dare, but I had feelings that got in my way. I had pride. I had territory I felt the need to protect.

But like most people, I also had feelings that would help me make up if I only heeded them. I had the need to keep a relationship in good shape. I found myself making up with Josselyn—and so many others—for no reason that I can remember.

I think the term "make up" gives a lovely clue to this mysterious part of forgiveness. Forgiveness is making up. It is made up; it requires imagination. We *make it up* out of misery and pain. Hurt and determined never, ever to forgive, we turn to our imaginations for help. We may find ourselves empathizing with the other person without intending to. Or we may suddenly see the situation in a new way. Or we may see ourselves in a different light. Then the dust of snow falls from a hemlock tree, and an amazing alchemy ensues.

The next thing we know, we have saved some part of a day we had rued. Pain changes into joy.

The stakes may be much higher than they were with Josselyn and our little spat.

I walked into an empty living room in Charleston, South Carolina, a few years ago, a room where, forty-five years before, I had often watched my stepfather attack my mother and me with a poker or just his bare hands. I grew up hating that man.

When I returned to that house, now a fifty-year-old man, and knocked on the door, I didn't know what I would find. I just wanted to revisit where I had lived and see how it looked and felt to me now. The kindly old gentleman who opened the door seemed immediately to understand what I had in mind when I told him I used to live in this house and wondered if I might look around. He stood aside, and, sweeping one of his arms toward the interior of the house, said, "Be my guest."

When I walked into the living room, the old scenes popped out at me as if in a hologram. I could see my stepfather right there, wearing his 100 percent cotton Brooks Brothers button-down oxford shirt with the gold collar pin beneath his tasteful tie. He would be mixing martinis at the table by the window, or sitting in his favorite chair, or yelling at me or my mother, or coming at her with a poker in his hand, always impeccably dressed. He even wore garters to hold up his socks. Men don't do that anymore. This was the 1950s.

As I took in the scene and let the memories click before my eyes, the place felt totally different now than it had back then. Now the room seemed small. I had remembered it as a huge, arch-ceilinged vault, holding my mother and me prisoners. But now, I was free. I was big now; the room was small. My stepfather was long gone. Only the hologram of my imagination could bring him back.

Curiously enough, the hatred I had felt for my stepfather wasn't there with me either. My stepfather had lost his power, much as the room had lost its size. Forgiveness had come out of hiding and was waiting to meet me where my stepfather used to sit. Forgiveness smiled at me, as if to say, "It's over now. It is safe to forgive him."

I began to forgive my stepfather that afternoon. He was dead, but my hatred had lived on. It started to die that day.

How? Why? I'm not sure. I had outgrown it. That day, I became open to forgiveness because I felt safe. Or maybe the kindly old gentleman who opened the door to the house was a wizard.

I hope you will find your equivalent of that kindly old man, perhaps in this book, opening a door to a special place, perhaps the most valuable, unpredictable place we humans ever go: the well-guarded land of forgiveness.

Question: What is your advice on teaching forgiveness to children? My eight-year-old just can't seem to grasp the concept of "moving on" from petty fights with his schoolmates.

Answer: This question is wonderful. While the ability to take revenge comes quite naturally to most children, the ability to forgive does not. It is important to teach it, at least as important as teaching reading or arithmetic.

But how? By far the best way is to model it yourself in your own life. Show your child how to forgive and move on by forgiving and moving on when you fight with your spouse, an in-law or a friend.

In addition to modeling forgiveness for your children, tell them about it. If they didn't see you fight with your friend and later forgive her, tell your eight-year-old how you did it. Put it in your own words.

For most people, moving on involves the three steps that a great teacher of psychiatry, Elvin Semrad, recommended: acknowledge what you are feeling—in this case anger, hurt and resentment, maybe with a dash of righteous superiority. Then bear (admit) what you are feeling, usually to another person—in this case your son. Then put the feelings into perspective. But you can't do that until you have done steps 1 and 2.

# 8

# Forgiving Yourself

The most difficult person to forgive is yourself. I have the
devil of a time forgiving myself, even when my life is
going just fine.

What have I done that's so bad? Lots of little things. A few
big things. No murders, but I have done an array of mis-
deeds, as have most people. Try as I might, I can't permanently rid myself of the guilt I carry.

There are, however, temporary means of relief. The way
out of guilt, the way to forgiving yourself as best you can,
was most unusually demonstrated to me by a cab driver in
Virginia.

When I got into his cab to go to the airport I had no idea
what a strange conversation I was about to have. This driver
looked to be in his late fifties. He had gray hair that flowed
out from beneath his cap, and he was wearing a very worn-
out brown leather jacket. He was smoking a cigarette, which,
as an ex-smoker, I thoroughly enjoyed.

We started talking, and I asked him if he had children. He
told me that he had two, both grown up and moved away.

Then I asked if he had grandchildren. "I don't know," was his surprising reply.

"Why don't you know?" I asked.

"I haven't talked to my kids in twenty years," he replied. "They don't want nothin' to do with me."

"Why?" I asked.

"Oh, they got good reasons," he replied. He spoke with a soft, southern accent, and he seemed like a gentle man. I wondered what terrible thing he could have done to drive his children away.

"You seem like a kind man," I said naively. "Couldn't you reconcile with your children?"

"No, I don't think so," he replied.

"Why not?" I asked.

"Because I hurt them too much," he replied.

I decided I had been too nosey as it was, so I stayed silent. However, this man wanted to say more. "I'm a transvestite, you see."

That was not on my list of possibilities. My image of transvestites had been shaped by my years in New Orleans in medical school and my visits to Provincetown in the summer. I didn't expect a leather-jacketed, cigarette-smoking, pale-faced, gray-haired cab driver in Virginia to tell me that he was a transvestite. "Oh," I said.

"I tried to control it for years, but I couldn't. Ruined my marriage. The kids were disgusted. They don't want to see me. I can understand."

"Who's in your life now?" I asked.

"Now I'm married to a wonderful woman who understands. She doesn't love it, but she loves me and she accepts it."

"You mean you cross-dress at home?"

"The minute I walk in the door," he replied enthusiastically. "These clothes come off and I put on my makeup and women's clothes. I feel like a new person then. The real me. I feel relaxed and glad to be alive. Wearing these clothes I'm wearing now feels so wrong. But, I've gotta have a job, and I can guarantee you my boss would fire me pretty fast if I came in dressed like a woman." He chuckled at the thought.

"You're very open about this," I said.

"Oh, I wouldn't have been a few years ago. My wife has helped me so much just by accepting me. She completely changed my life. She loves me. Me being a transvestite is not her preference, but she loves me anyway. And we have a great sex life, just in case you're wondering. We make love every day." I could see in the rear-view mirror that he was smiling at the thought.

"You're an amazing person," I said. "Thanks for being so open with me."

"My pleasure," he said. "Truly, it is. I am just so glad I *can* be open now. I wish I could forgive myself as much as my wife forgives me. But I'm getting there. Before she came into my life I hated myself totally. Now, I only hate myself a little, usually just when I think of my kids. But you know, I didn't choose to be this way, so why should I hate myself for being who I am?"

"You shouldn't," I said. "But you used to?"

"Yes, before my wife came along. I can't tell you how much that woman's love changed my life."

When we got to the airport, I gave him a big tip and got out of the cab. I leaned over and said through the passenger-side window, "Thanks. You really are an amazing man."

He looked up at me and said, "Aw, c'mon, don't tell me that!"

I laughed. "Okay, then, you're a spectacular woman."

"Now you're talking!" he replied with a big smile and blew me a kiss good-bye.

On my flight home I kept thinking about that man, the transvestite cab driver who was learning to forgive himself for being someone he couldn't help being.

Love allows us to forgive ourselves, more often than not, as it did for him. The hard part is finding that love. Often that love does not—will not, in spite of our best efforts—arise from within us. So then it must come from the outside: from a friend, a lover, perhaps a pet, or from that force some call God.

Forgiving yourself all by yourself is tough. I have seen people spend decades suffering from their own self-contempt, unable to find forgiveness from themselves. They never looked outside themselves because they didn't dare; they believed that others would scorn them even more than they scorned themselves. But they were never able to forgive themselves on their own, because forgiveness is usually an interactive process. When you need forgiveness for yourself, you need someone or something outside of yourself to inter- act with to make it possible.

If you choose the right kind of person, you will find that that person can help you simply by listening. Most of the time, your judgment of yourself is more severe than anyone else's. When you speak it out and let someone else hear, you start to feel better. The process of self-forgiveness can be slow, but it will begin once you connect with another person.

The reason others can help you in this way is simple. We're all in the same boat, just not all at the same time. We all need to be forgiven at some time or another. We all do bad deeds, at least once in a while. When you tell someone else something you feel guilty about having done, you touch a universal human nerve, the nerve of feeling bad for having done wrong. Some people will pretend that they don't have this nerve, and they will judge you harshly in an effort to distance themselves from you and what you've done. But they are blind. However, you must be careful not to choose such judgmental people to speak to about your shame and guilt. They'll only make you feel worse.

But if you choose someone who likes you and whom you trust, that person will feel close to you when you speak of what you believe you've done wrong, because that person will have been where you are. A circuit of forgiveness will develop between the two of you, and forgiveness will flow as if transfused.

Our need to be forgiven feeds our capacity to forgive, and our capacity to forgive derives from our need to be forgiven. When we talk about forgiveness we usually focus on one side or the other: granting forgiveness or seeking it. But, as I see it, each of those sides is a door into the same house, the house of forgiveness. When you grant forgiveness, you go through one door; when you seek it, you go through another. Both doors lead to forgiveness.

We all spend time trying to go through both doors. Each can seem locked at times. But the same key that gets you through one can help you get through the other.

If you have done something wrong, and you know you have done something wrong, you feel guilty. You are angry at yourself. You feel ashamed. You have not lived up to who you think you ought to be. You hope others will not see the you that you now see, the "real" you, the you that did the bad deed.

The longer you live with this shame and guilt without telling anyone about it, the more of a fraud you feel yourself to be. You carry with you the secret knowledge of how bad you are. No one else knows what you've done. In fact, everyone else might think you are quite wonderful, an upstanding citizen, a good father or mother, a good husband or wife, topnotch in your field, whatever. *But you know differently.*

The gap between how you see yourself and how the world sees you can widen into a chasm. Shame and guilt then haunt you, especially when you are alone. You may become depressed, turn to alcohol or some other kind of escape, or merely hate yourself.

You need forgiveness, but from whom? Will it help if you apologize to the person you hurt? Some traditions hold that this is the essential first step. But if you can't or you don't dare, you're stuck. And if the person to whom you apologize doesn't accept your apology, you may feel even worse. You still might be left with a residue of guilt and shame, a taint that can color your life forever.

There is a story of a man who felt so guilty over something he had done that he picked up a cross and carried it through a jungle terrain in Central America. People heard about this man, and as he would walk from village to village, they would offer him assistance, which he would refuse. One person commented as he saw the man, bent over, bleeding, gaunt with hunger, "Can't we tell him it's time to remove the cross? He has suffered enough."

Another bystander replied, "You know that. I know that. But he doesn't know it yet."

We who blame ourselves need to learn that we have suffered enough, and that further suffering only keeps us from doing good in the world. The man who carried the cross through the jungle in Central America helped no one by doing so, and he hurt himself a great deal. If you are angry with yourself, if you feel guilty, don't punish yourself. Reach out for love instead.

There is another obvious solution to guilt. The obvious solution is never to do anything you think is wrong. Of course, this is beyond us as humans. We all have done something we thought was wrong. Most of us have done many things we thought were wrong, and we continue to do them, day after day.

Interestingly enough, we also tend to judge others, day after day. I pass out summary judgments all the time, muttering to myself how stupid someone is, what a jerk someone else is, how rude that man is, how arrogant and full of herself that woman is, how contemptible some former friend has become. I don't publicize these judgments, but I make them internally all the time. And boy, do I enjoy doing it!

Yet how I cringe when I am judged. How I bristle, feel wounded or want to cry.

This process of judging and being judged is altogether human, and it will not soon end. But something useful can be learned by looking at the process: the reciprocity of forgiving

and the need to forgive. If we never needed forgiveness ourselves, it would be much more difficult to forgive others. But
because we all do need forgiveness, it helps to remember that
need of your own when you are judging someone else.

When the person in question is you, yourself, it helps to
turn to an intermediary.

I often tell my youngest son Tucker, who is seven as I write
this book, that he is "awesome." He usually replies, "Thanks,
Dad," or words to that effect.

One time, however, he said, "No, I am not. I am bad. I am
not awesome."

Tucker is an awesome kid, as are all kids, if you ask me.
Tucker has a blond buzz cut and a personality that is as bright
as his smile. He is the very picture of a lively and loving kid
if ever there was one. So, when he said he thought he was
bad, this was alarming.

At first I ignored him thinking perhaps he was joking or
imitating something he had heard. But as the days passed, he
persisted in calling himself bad.

I sat down with Tucker on his bed and asked him why he
kept calling himself bad. It turned out he was upset because
his older brother, Jack, was teasing him so much that he had
decided that it must be his fault. He had decided that he must
be bad.

Such was his love for Jack, so intense his desire for Jack to
be nice to him and play happily with him, that when he
couldn't control how Jack felt, he turned to what he could
control, his own feelings, and he blamed himself.

Thankfully, I could intervene and negotiate a better deal for
Tucker with Jack. Jack is just as good a kid as Tucker; he was

simply doing what older brothers usually do. And Dad could intervene.

Sweet, sad Tucker was doing what people of all ages do all the time: blaming themselves for what others do. They forgive everyone but themselves.

When what you have done is terribly wrong, when it is not in the category of Tucker's guilt but in the realm of appropriately severe guilt, there is still a way to forgive yourself, but such forgiveness usually requires an intermediary of some sort—real or imagined—to make the process interactive.

In July 1986, a twenty-two-year-old man named Bo Cox killed a man and received a life sentence for murder, to be served in a prison in the Midwest. I have never met Bo in person, but I have read some of his writings and I have spoken both to him and his wife, Deborah, on the telephone.

Bo was born in 1963 in a small town in Montana. His dad was a teacher in a one-room schoolhouse. After Bo's brother was born in 1968 the family moved to Wyoming where Bo's dad became a guidance counselor. When Bo reached the fourth grade the family moved once more, this time to a small town in Oklahoma. His dad continued to work in guidance in the public school there.

Bo loved his years in Oklahoma. His grandpa raised cattle there, so Bo developed a love of animals. He participated in 4–H and excelled in sports. He got good grades and was a generally happy kid. He went to the Episcopal church and served as an acolyte. His classmates said he had everything going for him. He certainly did not look like a future murderer.

However, there was a sadness in his family. His parents

split up when Bo was fourteen. Bo was required to go live with his mother, even though he would have preferred to live with his dad. Bo started to drink and smoke pot. His sadness, anger and confusion mounted. He stopped going to church. He managed to finish high school, but when he tried college his drug use—methamphetamine was now his staple—had become so severe that he couldn't keep up his grades, and he dropped out.

Now twenty-two and living at home, he was arrested twice for drug possession, but was given suspended sentences. He managed to get a job driving a dump truck for the county, all the while continuing his use of drugs and alcohol.

One night when he was drinking he got into a name-calling argument with some guy over a girl. The two of them began beating each other up. Quickly Bo was surrounded by his opponent's buddies. One of them, named Bart, jumped into the fight. Bo decided he better retreat since he was so badly outnumbered, so he ran to his truck and drove away.

However, as he was driving away he started to worry that people would mock him for running off. Then he made a decision that would change his life. He stopped at a friend's house and got a baseball bat and drove back to the scene of the fight. The others were all still there. Bo leaned out his truck's window and taunted them. They all said "Let's finish this right now." So the whole crew got into trucks and drove out of town where the police wouldn't interfere with their battle.

Once they reached their chosen battleground, Bo got out of his truck, bat in hand, and watched as his enemies drove by the spot. The one named Bart got out and came toward Bo. Bo lifted up his bat, swung and caught Bart square in the head. He didn't mean for that blow to kill Bart, but it did. A few hours later, Bo turned himself in to the police.

He was found guilty and sent to prison for life.

For four years, he continued to use drugs in prison ("It's sometimes easier to get drugs in prison than it is on the outside," he told me) as a means of dulling his emotions. Then, as he put it, "One day it was finally just too much. I was sitting on my bunk, wondering if this was all my life was ever going to be. That day I stopped doing drugs. My sobriety date is April 6, 1990."

For the first eight months he found abstinence "relatively easy," because he started to feel healthier right away. However, it was abstinence without much more than that. Then, on Christmas Eve, something amazing happened, something that once again would change Bo's life.

He attended a group-therapy meeting that Christmas Eve in prison, as he did every evening. But that night, in keeping with the holiday, all the men at the meeting joined hands and sang "Silent Night" together.

Suddenly, Bo felt a jolt. "I don't know what happened," he told me, "except right then and there I knew that God was real. Tears started to stream down my face—so I was real glad the lights were out and no one could see me crying. I know it sounds ridiculous, all these convicts in a circle holding hands, singing 'Silent Night' in the dark with the lights out, me crying over feeling that suddenly I know how real God is. But that's exactly what happened. I felt God saying 'I'm here and I'm real and everything's going to be okay.' Just the part that God was real shook me down to my feet because I hadn't ever *really* known that before."

Now he had a mission. He started writing for the prison newspaper, and he did it so well that he ended up winning a journalism award. He was even allowed to leave prison to attend the awards banquet. "People received me real well at the banquet," he told me. "I got my family back. They became proud of me again."

He also met Rev. Edward S. Gleason, editor of *Day by Day*, a bimonthly publication of daily meditations. Rev. Gleason invited Bo to write for *Day by Day*, which Bo did. His entry for Tuesday, May 21, 2001, took as its starting point a line from Psalm 5:5: "You hate all evildoers," then began his meditation for the day:

I would like to think the psalmist is talking about some *other* evildoer, not me. Sometimes I can even convince myself I'm not an evildoer, that what I did was an accident.

I write this in May 2001. I come up for parole next month. Fifteen years separate me from that night in 1986 when I killed Bart. Intentionally or not, what I did was take another man's life, cause him not to live anymore, kill him.

The parole board might ask, "Tell us why you think you deserve parole."

I've been tossing my answer around in my head for some time. I don't have a definitive response. I do know that I don't *deserve* parole. Or, if I do deserve it, I'm not the one to utter those words. Frankly, I don't have a leg to stand on. I am unable to defend myself and what I did, as well as being completely helpless to *undo* my actions.

People tell me all the time that God forgives me, but they say that until I learn to forgive myself, there's little chance I'll realize God's gift. I don't agree. God and I can both forgive me—even Bart's family might someday forgive me—and that won't bring Bart back.

I stepped across a holy and sacred line, into God's business. Life. I could understand if God hated me. Yet God doesn't. Crazy, huh?

Even though he feels forgiven by God, Bo still can't completely forgive himself. He knows that there are people who were close to Bart who have sworn to hate him for the rest of their lives. "I sometimes think that until I receive their forgiveness I can't forgive myself," he told me.

As someone who has worked so hard to find forgiveness and to deserve forgiveness, Bo is in a unique position to offer advice on how to forgive yourself. This is what he suggests: "Make amends. Then, live in such a way so as not to re-offend. The rest is time. It is an ongoing process. Every time something good happens I remember that Bart is part of it—that's how it has to be."

Bo Cox is one of the most impressive men I have ever encountered, and his wife Deborah is one of the most impressive women. She "met" Bo by looking at his photograph in a catalog that described various publications, among them *Day by Day*. She told me, "When I saw that photograph, I immediately knew that he was to be my husband. I called my brother-in-law and said, 'I've found my man. But there are two problems. He's in Oklahoma and he's in prison.'"

She wrote to Bo. A month later she drove to the prison to meet him. She drove sixteen hours through the night and stopped at a motel to shower. "I was excited," she said, "but I was worried that when he met me in person he wouldn't like me."

When Bo was brought out into the visiting area in the prison Deborah was thrilled. "I thought, *Wow! I did good!* He was so good-looking. We talked and walked all afternoon, outside with the flowers and the razor wire. There was no doubting in my mind, no question at all. We got married in prison. We had to get the marriage license with him in shackles and chains. That was hard."

They are still in love, still married and still hoping for parole, which was denied last time around.

You might be thinking, *But I have nothing in common with that man, Bo, or that woman, Deborah.* I disagree. I think we all have a lot in common with both of them.

What we have in common is that we've all made mistakes. And we all love people who have made mistakes. Bo made a huge mistake. Although you and I have not committed murder—or at least we haven't been caught—we have certainly done bad things. And we have wrestled within ourselves seeking forgiveness or trying to forgive.

You might even say you and I are also waiting for parole—from the judge within us, from God, or from whomever or whatever we imagine has the authority to grant us such parole. Oh, no, we don't wait every day as Bo and Deborah do. We don't wait in jail. We don't yearn to be with our spouses for just one day outside of prison.

But in a much milder version, don't we all hope for parole? Don't we all want to get off whatever hook we feel we're hooked on?

Bo found some peace of mind first by getting sober, then by feeling the reality of God in his life, then by falling in love. Each of us finds his or her own way, or it finds us. But if there is a unifying theme to most stories of self-forgiveness, be it in my son Tucker's life, in Bo Cox's life, in the life of the transvestite cab driver I met or in anybody's life, it is that by reaching out we best can change what lies within.

We gain parole by granting others what parole we can.

※　※　※

Just as this book was going to press, I got a note from Bo. It began, "On June 12, at 4:30 P.M., I walked out of the front doors of prison, got into a car with Debb and rode home. That's right. I'm out." His parole had come through. All the attempts to block it failed. After seventeen years in prison, Bo got his freedom back.

"Here are my plans as of today," he wrote.

I'm going to work in people's yards and other odd jobs. I'm fortunate there: I've never been afraid of work, and I even consider it a spiritual component (what's not?) of life. Not only that, I get to help Debb with the finances. Also, there's a ton of work to do around the house. Beyond that, I want to get *Free Spirit* out [his publication of spiritual reflections and meditations].

My first morning out, I walked out the front door and took off running. I ran three miles in one direction and three miles back. Let's just say it's difficult to sob

and gasp for air at the same time. Finally, I dried my
tears, held my head and ran like a free man. I was free
in prison—don't get me wrong—but I was surrounded
by razor-wire. Now, I'm surrounded by rabbits, deer,
fields, creeks, woods, cattle, birds . . . and a plethora of
other wildlife.

Last, please keep the Ennis family [the family of the
man Bo killed] in your prayers. I can't imagine what this
must be like for them. Now, if you'll please excuse me,
I've got to go wake Debb up for church.

I was stunned to receive Bo's letter. I had thought, as he
had thought, that he would be in prison, if not forever, at
least for a lot longer. Somehow the spirit of forgiveness
intervened.

I spoke to Bo on the phone the night before sending this off
to the publisher. He said to me, "I was with some friends
tonight and I had this quick feeling, like I had to catch my
breath. I said to myself, 'You are living in the middle of a
miracle.'"

# READER/CUSTOMER CARE SURVEY

We care about your opinions. Please take a moment to fill out this Reader Survey card and mail it back to us.
As a special "thank you" we'll send you exciting news about interesting books and a valuable Gift Certificate.

## Please PRINT using ALL CAPS

First
Name [_____] MI. [__] Last Name [_____]

Address [_____]

City [_____] ST [__] Zip [__][__][__][__][__]

Phone # ( [__][__][__] ) [__][__][__] — [__][__][__][__]    Fax # ( [__][__][__] ) [__][__][__] — [__][__][__][__]

Email [_____]

**(1) Gender:**
___Female    ___Male

**(2) Age:**
___12 or under    ___40-59
___13-19    ___60+
___20-39

**(3) Marital Status**
___Married
___Single
___Divorced/Widowed

**(4) Did you receive this book as a gift?**
___Yes    ___No

**(5) How many Health Communications books have you bought or read?**
___1    ___2-4    ___5+

**(6) How did you find out about this book?**
*Please fill in ONE.*
1) ___ Recommendation
2) ___ Store Display
3) ___ Bestseller List
4) ___ Online
5) ___ Advertisement
6) ___ Catalog/Mailing
7) ___ Interview/Review (TV, Radio, Print)

**(7) Where do you usually buy books?**
*Please fill in your top TWO choices.*
1) ___ Bookstore
2) ___ Religious Bookstore
3) ___ Online
4) ___ Book Club/Mail Order
5) ___ Price Club (Costco, Sam's Club, etc.)
6) ___ Retail Store (Target, Wal-Mart, etc.)

**(9) What subjects do you enjoy reading about most?** Rank only *FIVE.* Use 1 for your favorite, 2 for second favorite, etc.

|  | 1 | 2 | 3 | 4 | 5 |
|---|---|---|---|---|---|
| 1) Parenting/Family | ○ | ○ | ○ | ○ | ○ |
| 2) Relationships | ○ | ○ | ○ | ○ | ○ |
| 3) Recovery/Addictions | ○ | ○ | ○ | ○ | ○ |
| 4) Health/Nutrition | ○ | ○ | ○ | ○ | ○ |
| 5) Christianity | ○ | ○ | ○ | ○ | ○ |
| 6) Spirituality/Inspiration | ○ | ○ | ○ | ○ | ○ |
| 7) Business Self-Help | ○ | ○ | ○ | ○ | ○ |
| 8) Teen Issues | ○ | ○ | ○ | ○ | ○ |
| 9) Sports | ○ | ○ | ○ | ○ | ○ |

**(14) What attracts you most to a book?**
*(Please rank 1-4 in order of preference.)*

|  | 1 | 2 | 3 | 4 |
|---|---|---|---|---|
| 1) Title | ○ | ○ | ○ | ○ |
| 2) Cover Design | ○ | ○ | ○ | ○ |
| 3) Author | ○ | ○ | ○ | ○ |
| 4) Content | ○ | ○ | ○ | ○ |

TAPE IN MIDDLE; DO NOT STAPLE

FOLD HERE

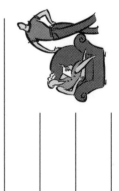

Comments:

*The student finds the Master asleep on a rock. He sits down near the rock and waits for the Master to wake up. He marvels at how soundly the Master is sleeping on such an uncomfortable bed.*

*In a few hours the Master wakes up. He spies the student sitting just a few feet away and asks, "Student, what do you want?"*

*"Master, I want to know how you can sleep so soundly on such an uncomfortable bed."*

*"Student, why do you bother to study with me? You are such a pitiful fool."*

*"Master, why do you ridicule me? I am merely trying to acquire your wisdom."*

*"Fool again! It is not my wisdom you seek, but wisdom itself. If you seek my wisdom you should go hang yourself, as I think you are a hopeless fool."*

*The student bites his tongue and forces back some angry words. Then he speaks. "I remember our previous lessons. I understand you are trying to teach me by what you are doing."*

*"If you remember our previous lessons, you will remember that I enjoy taunting you. Nothing is quite so much fun!"*

*The student now looks forlorn. He falls silent, as the Master sets about making a fire so he can boil some water for tea. Minutes pass during which nothing is said. Once the Master has made his tea, he sits down on the ground near the student. "Would you like some tea?" he asks.*

*"Yes, please!" the student replies.*

*"It would give me great pleasure," the Master says, "to throw my tea in your face. Then you would have some tea, and I would have the satisfaction of seeing a fool punished."*

*At that, the student gets up to leave. "I can see you do not care about me. I cannot learn from someone who doesn't care about me."*

*"Do you think life cares?" the Master asks sharply. "Do you think that rock I sleep on cares if it is soft enough for me? Why do you suppose I sleep on the rock? Not because I am a fool, but because I want to learn how to find comfort where there is little or none to be had. I am the rock you are trying to find comfort on. I am doing what life would do to you anyway, only I am doing it faster, and I speak back."*

*The student is pleased at this opportunity. "If you speak back, tell me, why should I not despise you, if you despise me?"*

*"For the same reason I embrace the rock. It's the only way I'll ever get a good bit of sleep."*

# 9

# How Not to Take It Personally

We can learn something from petty transgressions about how not to take it personally, whatever "it" is.

For example, look at how we deal with mosquitoes. A mosquito bite is a petty "transgression" that we have no trouble forgiving. Rare is the person who harbors a grudge against the mosquito that bit her. She tries to stop the harm the mosquito is doing—perhaps by trying to kill the mosquito—but unless she is out of her mind she does not carry on a personal vendetta with the mosquito.

What is the difference between how we deal with mosquitoes and how we deal with, say, the driver who stings us by cutting us off in traffic? Both the bite and being cut off qualify as petty offenses, but while we deal with a mosquito bite quite easily, being cut off in traffic can lead us to rabid responses. Why the difference?

Because we take being cut off personally.

When the mosquito bites us, we do not feel a loss of pride, a diminishment of self-esteem or anything of the kind. We feel annoyed, we feel a touch of pain, but we easily let that go. However, when someone cuts us off in traffic we can feel personally attacked—demeaned and diminished in our eyes and in the eyes of the world we imagine to be watching us. We feel a sudden desire to hurt the person who cut us off.

In fact, being cut off doesn't hurt us physically at all. Unlike the mosquito bite, this encounter does us no physical harm whatsoever, only psychological. If we are able to say to ourselves, *That's a bad driver,* or even, *What a jerk!* but not go the next step and feel personally affronted, then we will be able to forget the offense quickly and drive on in safety.

In so doing, we forgive the driver in the sense that we do not allow what he did to poison our own emotional system. We think he is a bad driver, maybe even a bad person; we believe he should be arrested, fined and maybe even sent to jail; but we stop short of letting him inject his poison into our bloodstream. We do not allow his "sting" to set off an inflammatory response within us. We are able to ward off the potentially lethal toxin his driving otherwise would have injected into us.

This is one way to define forgiveness: Do not allow what the other person did to poison your system. You don't allow it to get to you. You don't take it in and make it personal. You don't go on hating your ex-spouse forever or plotting revenge against your ex-boss indefinitely.

While you do not condone what was done to you, and you make every effort to prevent its being done again, you do not let the deed penetrate you and circulate throughout your emotional system like a venom.

You do not drive on entertaining violent fantasies against the driver who cut you off. You do not conjure up vile thoughts about his ethnic group or race or gender. You do not pursue him with the idea of pulling him over and smashing his skull with your tire iron. You do not pick a fight with your passenger as a way of displacing the anger you feel toward the driver who cut you off. You do not fall into a gloomy silence as you brood over the nastiness of mankind, the perils of modern life, the disappearance of politeness on the roads or the unfair consequences of being a nice guy. You simply chalk up being cut off to an encounter with a bad driver, even a jerk, not terribly unlike an encounter with a large, blood-sucking mosquito.

If you *do* take it personally, God help you—and everybody else around you. If you allow it, whatever it is, from mosquito to driver to any insult, to get to you, then you hurtle yourself into a place of immense danger. Suddenly, a minor insult sets off a chemical reaction in your brain. This reaction has led respectable people to commit murder. It has happened many times. The mildest insult can set off the most violent reaction.

For this reason, we need to inoculate ourselves and our children against taking it personally. Just as dangerous as polio was two generations ago, or AIDS is today, the get-even response kills millions each year around the world.

Let me offer a few steps you can follow in order to try not to take it personally and stave off the rage response:

- Admit you feel hurt and angry. This is usually pretty easy to do, but not always. Sometimes you will want to pretend it meant nothing to you. That is a mistake. You will only act on your anger later on.

- Grab for your psychological emergency brake. This has got to be very simple, as you do not have much time. A short phrase can work, like, "Don't do anything!" or "Remember last time!" or "Your life is at stake!" or "Don't be a jerk!" However you do it, you must stop yourself now. These split seconds—between when you feel the hurt and anger and when you decide what to do—tell the tale. You must understand that it is for your sake that you are holding back. Your life, your children's lives and the lives of all the people you love can be ruined in split seconds. You must be able to shut yourself down, or you might die.

- Once you have prevented murder or some milder equivalent, it is time to *think.* This is one time you do not want your emotions to guide you. You want reason to take charge. *Think* about how much better off you will be by not taking what the idiot did personally. *Think* how much better off you will be by exercising control. *Think* how proud you will be of yourself, and others of you, that you didn't lose it. Think how much money you'll save. *Think* how many days in the hospital or in court you won't have to spend. *Think.*

- As you have been thinking, your physiology has most likely been resetting itself at a calmer place. Now you can relish what you've done. You have held back. You have not taken it personally. You have done well. Give yourself rewards for this. Drive on and smile.

But what about punishment for the offending party? Recklessly taking revenge may lead to disaster, but how about taking revenge judiciously? Isn't that justice? If society lets people cut in line, steal parking spots or the many equivalent deeds, then pretty soon we will no longer have a society. We need rules and laws, and we need the ability to enforce the rules and laws.

But do we need vengeance? Do we need to satisfy that desire for retribution that flares up in almost all of us when we are wronged? Vengeance may be the most destructive of all desires. Do we need to satisfy it, like an irresistible, monstrous sweet tooth? A sweet tooth for revenge can be the death of us.

I took vengeance against the man who took my parking spot, and in so doing I thought I was taking vengeance against entitled BMW owners everywhere—as well as everybody else who has more than I do and lords that fact over me. That bit of vengeance felt good to me. To tell the truth, it even feels good now retelling it. It feels good to see bad guys get back what they dish out.

But it is also something I hope to never do again. I risked my life, the driver's life, his passenger's life, not to mention the lives of the children we all might have and the feelings of the people who love us. (Yes, I will concede that there was probably someone in this world who loved the loathsome driver of that BMW, not to mention his perhaps not-loathsome passenger.)

But in satisfying my desire for revenge, I was not enforcing any law. I was not protecting society, nor was my revenge in any way meaningful. My victim learned nothing from it, and his only response to me was hardly satisfying, namely showing me his middle finger. All I did was satisfy my craving for that man's figurative scalp. I wanted suddenly to hurt him, and, more than that, to see him squirm. I wanted to do exactly what I did: to sit above him, as I imagined he and his kind had always sat above me; make him squirm, as he and his kind had always made me squirm; and finally get my way, as he and his kind had always had theirs.

I wanted my moment of superiority. I wanted my moment of control. I wanted to be king and decree whose head was to be chopped off.

At that moment, justice was the last thing on my mind. I could rationalize it and call it justice, but it was something much more instinctual. I wanted to rub his face in all the humiliation he had rubbed so many other faces in, including mine. But my motive was not even that noble. Really, what I wanted was what we all want. I wanted to get my own way.

I lucked out. I got what I wanted. But my life could easily have ended that night on a hot street in New Orleans. Lives end that way every day.

In the name of justice, I took personally an insult that was not meant personally. I allowed my anger to flare up out of control. The guy just wanted a parking space. He didn't want *my* parking space, he wanted *a* parking space. By taking it personally, I endangered lives. But what about justice? Don't we have a right to expect that? Isn't vengeance sometimes justified? Of course. But forgiveness and punishment are not incompatible. I can forgive—that is, renounce my anger and resentment toward—the crooks who ransacked my hotel room once, but still endorse their being punished.

Sometimes, however, we use the concept of justice to justify an onslaught of anger.

Question: After many unsuccessful attempts to tell a manipulative friend why his behavior bothers me, I've decided to end our friendship, but I don't want to be malicious. How can I end this friendship without angering him?

Answer: You can't control his response.

You have reached a point where you are saying, "I have tried to tell you how I need for you to change if I am going to enjoy being your friend. Since you have not changed, I no longer enjoy being your friend, so I want to stop being in contact with you."

In doing this I would be less concerned about angering him than leaving you with a lingering resentment or even a grudge. If you carry a grudge, remember that you are the one who carries the poison.

One way to get past your resentment is to forgive him for being who he is. You just have to give up on the hope that he will be different from who he has been all along.

It is not fair to you, or to him, to carry on a friendship weakened by conditional caring. "I would like you a lot," you say, "if you were not so manipulative. But since you are manipulative and will not heed my requests to change, I do not like you enough to remain your friend."

Now try rephrasing it in your mind, as follows: "Your manipulative behavior has hurt me several times, and I am angry about that. However, I must accept that a manipulative person is who you are. I am working on letting go of my hope that you will change, which is to say, I am working on forgiving you for being who you are."

If you can say that to yourself, then you do not necessarily have to stop being his friend. If you can accept his bad with his good, you can stay his friend. But if you can't, then you can let go of him as a friend without holding a grudge (which is a masked desire that he will change) or worrying about his being angry with you (which is a masked version of your inability to forgive yourself for being angry with him).

# 10

# A Lover's Quarrel: Or, When They Know Not What They Do

**I** have a friend, whom I'll call Polly, whose husband is a surgeon. They are both good people, not inclined toward violence. But one evening Polly came home to find her husband, whom I'll call Jeff, in a rage. A patient of his had filed a malpractice suit against him, and he was fuming. As Polly tried to talk to him and offer him comfort, Jeff became angry at Polly, even though she was only trying to help him feel better. The more she tried to console him, the angrier he got. "What do you know about what I'm going through?" he yelled at her. "You're so stupid. You'd never understand."

"Jeff, don't call me stupid," Polly said.

"Then don't be giving me these lame, stupid clichés. You can't help me, so don't bother to try."

"Why are you pushing me away?" Polly asked.

"Because you can't help me. You don't even care about helping me. All you want is what I can give you. You don't really care about me. You are just another social climber. All you care about is my prestige and my money."

I saw Polly the next day. She told me about the lawsuit,

and then she repeated verbatim the words Jeff had spoken to her. What he said had really rocked her. "He's never been mean to me like that," she said. "He insulted me over and over again, really nasty insults, and nothing I said seemed to help. Today I feel hurt and distant and out of love."

"You've been married a long time," I replied. "This has never happened before?"

"No, never. We've had arguments, but nothing even close to this one."

We talked for a while. Polly understood that Jeff had been irrational and upset over the lawsuit. "But what does that mean about him? That from now on whenever he gets upset he will turn on me like that? Does he really believe deep down what he said about me? I can't live with that. I am so angry with him, I can't even look at him, but I am also afraid of him. That's a bad combination."

One of the harshest truths about human nature is that we lash out at those we are closest to. Jeff had lashed out at Polly in a mean and insensitive way. Was forgiveness here appropriate, let alone possible? Did it even matter that Jeff hadn't really meant what he said and wasn't himself when he said it?

I talked to an older friend of mine—I'll name him Ken—who has been practicing psychiatry for about forty years. I told him about Polly and Jeff and asked his advice. Ken took a deep breath, let it out, and then he smiled a rueful smile. "I work with lots of couples and families," he said. "And I see this all the time. Often it gets violent. The basic deal of someone hurting someone else when they feel hurt themselves? It happens every day, all the time, I'm sad to say."

"What do you do about it?" I asked.

"First I listen. People need to be heard. Get the anger out there on the table. And the truth needs to be told, at least each person's version of the truth. Sometimes that's all they'll let me do. But, if they'll let me do more, I try to see if a bridge can be built. Take your friend, Polly, for example. Does she really love Jeff, do you think?"

"Yes, I've known them for years. Polly is very strong and so is Jeff, so they can spar when they're together, but they have always seemed to care a lot for each other, and I know they love their kids a lot," I replied.

"So there is something there worth saving?" Ken asked.

"Oh, yes, very much so," I replied.

"I don't know," Ken said. "People walk out pretty easily these days. They might break up."

"But why do you think Jeff lost it as much as he did?" I asked. "He's never done that before."

"You want me to sound like a shrink?" Ken asked with a little wink. He had white hair and the kindest, wisest blue eyes I've ever seen. Those eyes had seen it all, or so I imagined.

"Yes, please, tell me what you think."

"Well, your friend, Jeff, had just gotten notice of being sued. This had never happened to him before, so I am sure he felt debased in his own eyes and in the eyes of others." I nodded. "So, when he got home, he was furious. He was all worked up. When he saw Polly, he wanted her to feel what he was feeling, so he wouldn't have to feel it alone. That's why he tried to make her feel as low and devalued as he felt."

"Aw, c'mon, Ken," I said. "He didn't insult her like that as a way of sharing his feelings."

"Yes," Ken said, "that's *exactly* what he did. He didn't do it consciously, but the force that made him do something that he had never done before was his desire to bring his wife into his own agonized state of mind. This is primitive stuff. It is not an intellectual, well-considered decision. And for educated people like your friends, this is a means of discourse they very rarely get into. That's why it was so new. But what your friend Jeff was doing was making sure his wife felt what he was feeling. I'm right about this, Ned. I see it almost every day."

"Even if it's true what you say," I replied, "what can I tell Polly to do?"

"Tell her not to take it personally," Ken said. "Of course you might get a black eye if you do tell her that, but that's what she needs to hear and then do, one way or another. That's the key to it all. Don't take it personally."

"But how can she not?" I protested. "He said really mean things about her."

"Yes," Ken said, "and that's why I say they might split up. She is in the right, he is in the wrong; she has hurt feelings, he did a terrible thing. What is the 'correct' thing to do? Maybe it is to get Polly out of there. Break up the marriage. Move on to someone else."

"But you don't sound like you really think that's for the best," I said.

"You're right, I don't. But who am I? I'm just an aging shrink, probably out of step with the times. I think if your friends love each other and they love the kids, they should stay together. Life dishes out lots of harsh blows. I don't know of many long-term marriages that haven't included a bad fight. I bet they'll both regret it if they split up, not to mention the impact on their kids. I think they could make things right between them, if Jeff works hard at it and if Polly can understand deep in her heart that Jeff didn't mean what he said."

"If she can hang in there, you think they'll get to a better place?"

"I'd bet on it," Ken said. "Most people may not give their spouse as bad a time as he did that night, but *everyone* dumps their pain on their spouse or whoever else they can find who's close to them. We all do it. We don't do it on purpose. In fact, we try hard not to do it. But we just can't help it. We do it unconsciously. We do it in spite of ourselves. Some people call it original sin. Some people call it projective identification. Whatever you call it, you need to know it exists, otherwise you'll never understand people. You'll think most people are bad, instead of just human."

"But that doesn't mean you give people an excuse to be cruel, does it?" I asked.

"Of course not," Ken replied. "But it does mean you cut people some slack for being human. Instead of getting up on your high horse and pointing out faults wherever you find them, you admit that we're all flawed. That is to say, we're all human, and we're all destined to hurt one another, even though we don't want to and we don't mean to. We all dump on each other. We all give each other a hard time one way or another. The only way out of this mess is to learn how to forgive, which means not to take things so damn personally. Then you don't have to get even, or stomp around in anger, or break up, or do all the other things people do when they get hurt. We all hurt each other. So we just have to hang in there with each other and try to be smart and patient enough so that we don't end our lives all alone, having rejected everybody by then."

As it turned out, Jeff and Polly stayed together, and they are happy today. I never relayed Ken's advice to Polly, but a couple of years later she did say to me, "He was crazy when he did it. He wanted to make me feel as bad as he was feeling." Polly had come to the very same conclusion Ken had reached.

Polly found the hook within her. She was able—over time—to renounce her feelings of anger and resentment toward Jeff. First she expressed the anger, then she talked about it, then empathy began to build that bridge Ken was talking about.

She never explicitly articulated all that Ken had hypothesized, that Jeff was trying to make her feel what he was feeling, but she was at least able to overcome her feeling that Jeff was dangerous. She was able to regain her feeling of safety, as well as her love for Jeff.

The process Ken was describing has a name among psychiatrists; as mentioned, it is called projective identification. Maggie Scarf has written brilliantly about it for lay readers in her book called *Intimate Partners*.

One example of its therapeutic use is in psychotherapy. Often, patients unconsciously project their negative feelings onto the therapist. The therapist does not respond by getting angry or resentful. Rather, he "holds" the negative feelings for the patient; as he holds them, they gradually become less toxic. The patient begins to feel better. By not returning

negative feeling with negative feeling, by not taking personally what the patient is doing, the therapist transforms the
feelings from something toxic into something bearable, if not
pleasant. The therapist does not explicitly forgive the patient,
but what he does makes the patient feel forgiven. The
patients do not know what they are doing as they project
their negative feelings onto the therapist; you could say that
they know not what they do. But the therapist, by not
responding with hostility, by not taking it personally, changes
the quality of what has been projected.

In this way, one person's taking on the toxic feelings of
another can make the other person better. If the therapist
knows how to take care of himself, he does not get hurt,
either.

A more violent example comes from the Bible: the story of
the crucifixion. You do not need to be Christian or subscribe
to any religious belief for this example to make sense. Just
consider the story, as it has been told in the New Testament.

The chief priests crucified Jesus because he became too
important. They envied him, as we all have envied someone.
But they were not ordinarily envious; they were mad with
envy. They therefore craved an extreme remedy, just as Jeff,
the surgeon, had been mad with anger and sought an
extreme remedy. They projected their own hostile, hateful
feelings onto Jesus, thereby turning him into a dangerous
man guilty of blasphemy and deserving of death, in their
eyes. So they demanded that he be put to death.

Whether or not you believe in the divinity of Christ,
whether or not you think Jesus was the Son of God, you
would still agree that he had the ability to fight back if he had

chosen to. But he did not fight back. He allowed himself to be betrayed, tried, convicted and crucified, all without putting up any physical resistance.

Crucifixion is one of the most painful ways to kill a person. The person being crucified twists in agony, slowly losing his ability to breathe, as his lungs fill up and he starts to drown in what little fluid he has left in his baked body. Even in such extreme pain, Jesus cried out, as he was on the cross, "Forgive them, Father, for they know not what they do." Whether or not you believe that Jesus was divine, what he said on the cross is one of the most extraordinary examples ever recorded of empathizing with the people who have hurt you.

Having been betrayed by a disciple, and while suffering extreme humiliation and physical pain, Jesus pleaded for the forgiveness of those who were torturing him to death. He did not plead for his own life—even in such extreme agony—but he pleaded for the lives and souls of the very people who were inflicting the pain.

Jesus could bear the pain because he didn't take personally the torture he received. He could bear the pain others were inflicting without needing to hurt those people in return. Jesus didn't get seduced by a desire for retribution. He accepted the worst mankind has to offer without wanting to return it in kind. He broke the chain of retribution, and in so doing transcended the automatic process of revenge.

Whether his doing that saved humankind or not, and whether his spirit lives on even after his death, is a matter of theology. My point is psychological. I am citing Jesus' crucifixion as an ultimate example of extreme injustice and physical suffering not being taken personally.

For such a deed to have the miraculous impact Christians believe it did, greater powers than those we understand must have taken over. But let's leave the divine influence out of this discussion, and just look at it from a human, psychological point of view. Christians often say Jesus died to save us. How could Jesus' death—or anyone's death—save anyone else's soul? How can one person—like you or me—be forgiven on account of the torture, suffering and death of another person?

When a person accepts injustice, pain and suffering without shooting back injustice, pain and suffering in return, something unusual happens. Hatred collides with forgiveness, like matter colliding with anti-matter. One cancels out the other. When a person who is subject to the seemingly unstoppable laws of human nature that we all are subject to does not obey those laws, we all are affected by it.

No one acts in isolation. The least deed any of us does affects all the rest of us, sometimes in a minuscule, immeasurable way; sometimes in a majestic, obvious way. But just as a sneeze in New York affects the wind in Peru, the smallest act any of us commits registers somewhere, somehow on the global field of human energy.

Routine acts of hatred followed by other routine acts of hatred keep the winds of meanness blowing strong. But when someone interrupts that cycle by absorbing the blow without retaliation, the winds, for a moment, change.

Jesus is only the most famous example in Western tradition. In a secular, psychological sense, we see people every day doing what Jesus did; people who resist the temptation to return hurt with hurt, blame with blame, and hate with hate may even go so far as to say words that approximate,

"Forgive them, for they know not what they do."

Let me give you the most common example that I can think of. Every day, children say to one parent or another, "I hate you!" Every day all over the world, children kick, slap or otherwise attack their parents. While parents may punish or otherwise put an end to such behavior, they usually do so lovingly. They usually do not return the hateful words or actions with hateful words or actions of their own, because they know the transgressors are only children, after all, and their children at that. The hatred ends right there.

If we could extend to each other the same empathy we extend to our own children, forgiveness would come more easily. We should do this. We are all children after all. We are all a long way from grown up.

When one of us is strong and patient enough to accept pain, injustice and suffering without returning it in kind, we all benefit. We all have our spirits raised, and our collective rage diminished, perhaps only as little as a sneeze in New York affects the wind in Peru, but that much, at least.

The reason, then, that one person's suffering can relieve the suffering of others is that one suffering person blocks the relentless current. The one person is doing something rare: exchanging revenge for empathy, exchanging hatred for love. Think back to what Hannah Arendt wrote: "Forgiving . . . is the only reaction which does not merely re-act but acts anew and unexpectedly, unconditioned by the act which provoked it and therefore freeing from its consequences both the one who forgives and the one who is forgiven."

As he hung on the cross and begged for the forgiveness of those who were torturing him, Jesus broke the cycle of anger and revenge. He acted in a new and unexpected way. He rose above the human response and gave us all an example to which we can aspire.

But even if Jesus did that, we might wonder how his suffering and his forgiving could save anyone else—like you or me.

Or, to bring the example back to our contemporary world, how could Polly's suffering Jeff's unjust, cruel words lead to something good not only for Polly but for Jeff as well? We might as well include all of us in the example, as we have all hurt others at one time or another. Then the question becomes this grand question: How does any one person's forgiving injustice committed by another person help us all?

By pointing the way out of the mess we are in.

Look out at the world. Look at us all, how hurt we are. Look out at us all, carrying around our wounds and injustices, trying to get back at others, trying to get even, trying to scratch out a living.

Like Jeff, the surgeon, we all tend to inflict our pain upon one another whether we mean to or not. We all tend to work out our conflicts upon the backs of each other, especially our friends. We all have been unfair and mean.

If we can look beyond the deed a person does, and wish for something other than blame, if we can wish for understanding, as Jesus did on the cross, as Buddha seems to have done all the time, and as we ordinary others sometimes do, as Polly did, as we all *can* do, we can begin to forgive everyone, and we can begin to forgive ourselves. We can begin to find a way out of the inexorable cycle of bad deed after bad deed.

It is possible. It is difficult and strange and maybe seems stupid, but it is possible.

# 11

# Forgiving Your Ex

**W**hen two people break up, the fallout from the blast can last for years, even a lifetime. Whether the break-up is in marriage, romance, business or friendship, it is common for both parties to wage war for a long, long time.

While understandable, this is a colossal waste of time. It is also toxic and bad for everyone involved. When children are involved the situation can be tragic. These innocent kids can be as badly burned as if they were hit by napalm. We should do all we can to prevent such damage.

As one who was victim of two divorces when I was a child, I long ago forgave the people involved. I just wish the first divorce never had happened. (I was grateful for the second one.) My parents' divorce was easily the worst event of my life. However, I am grateful that my parents did not wage war with each other for very long. In fact, my father sent my mother a dozen pink roses on her birthday every year, even after both of them had remarried. And, when my father was dying, my mother drove from her house on Cape Cod up to New Hampshire to visit him in the hospital so she could fluff up his pillows one more time and say good-bye to the man who was truly the love of her life.

They managed to forgive each other, although both of them held a quiet grudge. My mother divorced my father because he went crazy, and then she took up with another man. When my father got better—he was put on Lithium and essentially cured of his illness—he resented my mother for not waiting for him to get better. She told him that the doctors said he never would get better, which indeed they had said, but my father still resented her for having left him. Nonetheless, they forgave one another enough to remember the good times and let those memories dominate. They didn't let anger and resentment take over their feelings for each other. The pink roses came every year, and my mother was at my father's bedside at the very end.

It often works the other way.

I hate him. I always will hate him. How could he have done that to me? Every time I think of him with that stupid little bimbo, I want to kill him. He's running around with her while I am home cleaning up vomit and doing laundry. How could I ever have been so dumb as to have married him in the first place? Oh, he was so smooth when we were dating. He said *all* the right things, how he wanted a stable family, how he liked to spend quiet time at home and relax, how he would always love me no matter what. It was all a great big lie! Why didn't I see it?

Edie spent many sessions talking to me like this about

Sam, her ex-husband. Now she was a single mom, raising three teenagers, living off alimony and child support, as well as what she earned as a freelance editor working out of her home. She was a lovely, kind and very intelligent woman. Her hatred for Sam stood in contrast to the rest of her emotional makeup.

After a while, it seemed to me that listening to her detail her reasons for hating Sam was becoming counterproductive, so I ventured a risky opinion. "Edie, don't you think all this anger toward Sam might be a way for you to stay connected to him?"

"What do you mean?" she snapped. "You think I want any part of that creep? Well, of course, you wouldn't really understand. You're a man, too."

"I am a man," I replied, "but I also am a person. And a person who likes you and doesn't like to see what all this anger is doing to you."

"You like me?" Edie said, looking up.

"Yes, I like you. You know that, don't you?"

"Yes, I guess I know that. It's just that no one has said that to me in a long time," she said.

"Well, do you think that might be because you are so wrapped up in anger that it is hard for people to bring out the part of you that they like?"

"But what am I supposed to do?" she pleaded. "I used to love him so, so much. And then he just walked all over that. He spit on it. He might as well have taken a knife and cut me up. All I'm left with is hatred. If it weren't for the kids, I'd think seriously about suicide."

"But, Edie," I said, "I'm not saying your hatred for Sam

isn't real or justified. Just that it is eating you up. He might as well be using that knife on you right now, the way your hatred is cutting you up."

"But what can I do about it?" Edie asked. "It's what I feel. I can't just stop feeling what I feel. I wish I could. Oh, how I wish I could."

"I think you can," I interjected. "I think if you really want to get past your anger toward Sam, you can."

"I want to," Edie said. She sat in silence for a moment and started to get tears in her eyes. "I guess I want to. But I love him. If I stop hating him, I won't have him at all."

"You won't have him in the destructive way you have him now," I replied. "Now, all you have is this nasty version of him that is making you depressed and angry. Don't you think it would be good to let go of that?"

"But what will I have left? Nothing. Nothing. I will be empty."

"No, you won't," I countered. "You will be free. And you'll feel much more full of what you want to feel full of. You will also be ready to meet someone else you might really love."

From there we started working on forgiving Sam. I carefully defined "forgive" for Edie as letting go of anger and resentment. She did not need to condone what he had done, she did not need to pretend he hadn't hurt her—and hurt her worse than she ever had been hurt. All she needed to do was let go of her last attachment to Sam, her rage and resentment.

We used many of the steps I outlined in chapter 7. We didn't go through them one by one, as that is not the way the process of forgiveness works. But we did touch on many of them.

To remind you, these are the steps I suggested using:

## Act I: Pain and Hurt
### Scene:

1. You suffer some kind of hurt.
2. Live through the flood of emotion. This takes time.
3. Talk to other people you trust.
4. Don't withdraw from life. Stay connected.

## Act II: Reliving and Reflecting
### Scene:

5. Appeal to your beliefs.
6. Grieve the loss of whatever this wrong robbed you of.
7. Look for the hook that makes you unable to forgive.
8. Consider how you might possibly be acting like a fool.
9. Do what you need to do to regain your feeling of safety and control.
10. Empathize with the person or people who hurt you.

## Act III: Working It Out
### Scene:

11. Wrestle within yourself to flatten the hook.
12. Think; use insight.
13. Pray or meditate upon the situation.
14. Give thanks for what you have.
15. Imagine vengeance.
16. Focus on the future.
17. Remind yourself that you and the world will be better off if you forgive.
18. Remind yourself that you need forgiveness, too.

## Act IV: Taking Stock and Moving Forward
### Scene:

19. Renounce your anger and resentment.
20. Repeat these steps as often as you need to until the hook stays out and the anger is gone.
21. Be nourished by this act of forgiveness and grow from it.
22. Help others in their efforts to forgive.

At first, Edie focused on steps 1 through 4. The initial phase was the flood of emotions she felt after being betrayed by Sam. Then she began to talk to her friends about it, and to talk to me. At my urging, she countered her desire to withdraw by resuming her work editing, as well as going to the health club, and she joined a women's dinner group at the invitation of one of her friends. Remaining connected is a very good way to counteract the deluge of toxic feelings that being alone and doing nothing can create.

Steps 5 and 6 also helped Edie. She really did believe in forgiveness. Although she was brought up Jewish, she was no longer religious, but she deeply believed in trying to do what is right. Her beliefs led her to want to get beyond her anger and resentment toward Sam, if she could.

Step 6, in fact, was key. She needed to grieve the loss of Sam. She had loved him totally, and still sort of did. He was once the perfect man in her eyes, and her perfect man to boot. She now needed to feel how horribly sad she was to have lost that version of Sam. This step took a while.

Step 12 also helped a lot. Edie was very bright and she profited from thinking things through. She understood intellectually that it was bad for her and for her kids to go on hating Sam. Being highly intelligent, she didn't want emotion to overrule her judgment. This was a struggle, as she was an emotional, passionate woman. But she was determined not to allow herself to "let him win," as she put it, by rendering her permanently angry.

Steps 14 and 15 also helped. A few fantasies of revenge warmed Edie's heart and made us both laugh. And giving thanks for the good in her life helped her focus on the future. She had three great kids and financial security, and she had her lively, vibrant self.

Gradually, she was able to renounce her anger and resentment. It was never gone completely, but it didn't dominate her world as it had before. She still thought of Sam as a "total jerk," but she didn't need to bring him up much, nor did she think about him much when she was alone.

You could see how her forgiving Sam had nourished her. She stood taller, she laughed more, she was quicker with the witty repartee, and even her skin took on a healthier glow. She was much better off when she let go of her angry attachment to Sam.

She also became very good at helping her friends who were going through bad divorces. "Don't let the bad guys win," was her refrain. "Good riddance. Let him go. Live well. That's what will really kill him!"

Of course, she wasn't living well in order to kill Sam; that would not truly have been living well. We often imagined, though, how surprised Sam must have been at how healthy and happy Edie had become only a year after the divorce. "He didn't think I could do it," she said triumphantly in our last session. "I am so much happier now than I've ever been. Thank you."

"You're welcome," I said. "And let me thank you. I have enjoyed our time together." And so we said good-bye.

I believe that anyone can do what Edie did. Not only can do, but should do. Why waste your time and damage your health by seething with anger and dreaming of revenge? When Edie said she'd like to stop doing that but didn't know how, I knew she could learn how. What holds people back from forgiving is that they don't really want to forgive.

The same principles apply to getting past our anger at anyone we once liked or loved, such as a friend, a boss, a partner or even an institution, like a company, church or synagogue.

Just refer to the process and work through it in whatever order makes sense for you, skipping the parts that don't seem useful. If you have trouble, a therapist or a trusted friend can make the process much more effective.

Question: How can I begin to untangle a family feud that has been in effect for years?

Answer: Be careful. If you are going to try to untangle the family feud by yourself, the odds are not only that you will fail but you will get hurt to boot.

It is a more realistic undertaking to instigate the whole family to work to untangle the family feud. In other words, try to set in motion a process that will involve as many other members of the family as possible in taking ownership of the problem and solving it.

Families don't like to change. That is why they

continue the same fights not only for lifetimes, but generation after generation. "I don't know why I hate my Uncle Bill, I just do. My father hated him, just as my grandfather hated his brother. We'll never get along. I'm sure our children won't either. It's in our blood." Those lines are written in many families.

To oppose a family's desire to fight is to oppose one of the great pleasures of life: righteous indignation. All parties feel *sooooo gooood,* being so right about their respective positions.

Furthermore, to oppose a family's desire to fight is also to encourage a feeling most people resist at all costs: the feeling of vulnerability. When you begin to say perhaps you were wrong, that perhaps the other person's position has some merit to it, you begin to feel less in control, more vulnerable and therefore more afraid.

Most of us cover our fears very quickly with anger. Anger takes us out of the fearful, vulnerable position and puts us back into attack mode, which restores our feeling of control, as well as reducing our feeling of vulnerability.

So, when you oppose the family feud—or the feud of any large group—you are playing with nuclear weapons, emotionally speaking. Be careful.

I suggest consulting with an expert, if you are really serious about this. Family therapists have a lot of experience in defusing bombs. They know when to cut the red wire and when to cut the green.

Also, they are not part of the bomb themselves, as you or I would be in our own family feuds.

It takes immense skill and more than a short time to permanently defuse the bomb of a long-standing feud. Look at the history of the Middle East, if you need convincing.

# 12

# Forgiving Those Who Hurt Us ...
# and Who Won't Apologize

I sat across from Louise, a fifty-two-year-old woman, as she told me of her dilemma. "My mother is dying. I don't know how many more months she has. My problem is that I hate her. I can tell you in great detail why I hate her, if you'd like to know. But that isn't why I am sitting here in a psychiatrist's office." She paused and looked down at my rug with its fanciful designs of circus animals and sprites. The rug was a gift from my wife.

"So, why did you come to see me?" I asked.

"Because for the first time in my life I have no idea what to do. My mother is dying, I hate her, and I don't know what to do next."

"Why do you have to do anything?" I asked.

"Because, if she dies and nothing has changed, I fear that I will feel horrible for the rest of my life."

"Why will you feel horrible?" I asked, practicing the art of what my old teacher, Tom Gutheil, called "clinical dumbness." The idea is to ask the question, no matter how dumb it sounds, to try to help the patient expand on the problem in her own terms.

"That is a stupid question," Louise appropriately responded. "I was told you are a good shrink, not the mechanical wind-up toy your profession is so full of."

"I'm sorry," I replied. "I didn't mean to be stupid. I think I know why you'll feel horrible, but I don't want to assume that I know what you think and feel. After all, we're only just getting to know each other."

"I'm so irritable," Louise responded. "I am obviously distraught. I am not used to feeling this way. I am used to being in control. I am used to knowing what to do. The fact is, I don't know the answer to your question. Maybe that's why it annoyed me. I suppose I'll feel horrible if she dies and nothing has changed because I will feel guilty that we never made up."

"Or maybe also because the chance that someday you might make up will be gone?" I ventured.

"Aren't they the same things?" Louise asked.

"I guess so," I replied, hoping I hadn't irritated her once more. "It's just that when she dies, a certain hope you have harbored for years might die with her. The hope that things between you will change."

"They'll never change," Louise said glumly. "I don't have that hope now, and she is still alive. She is as mean and stubborn as they come."

"And yet you say you'll feel horrible when she dies."

"I don't want her to die," Louise said. "God knows why, but I don't want her to die. She is such a part of my life. I'll miss her, the way I miss weeds when I pull them out."

"She's your mother," I said. "Children love even the worst mothers."

"Don't get carried away," Louise interrupted with a

chuckle through her tears. "I've hated her for as long as I can remember."

"Do you really cry when you pull out weeds?" I asked.

"No, not literally. But, yes, in a funny sort of inner way, I do cry when I pull out weeds. I guess I just hate saying good-bye to anything."

"Do you think that's the sum of it, then?" I asked. "You'll feel horrible when your mother dies because as much as you hated her, you'll hate to say good-bye to her, and because you're accustomed to having her around, you'll miss her?"

"That's a lot of it," Louise said, looking back down at the rug, dabbing her eyes with a Kleenex she took from her purse. "But that's not, as you say, the sum of it. There's more." I remained silent, as she seemed to be thinking, and I didn't want to distract her with questions. In a few moments she began to fill in some of the blanks. "Why couldn't I change her? Why didn't she love us all enough to change herself? Why was she so selfish? Why did she hurt me so much and make me who I am? Why can't I just let her go?"

"Good questions," I replied. "Hating her binds you to her, maybe?"

"But I can't stop hating her," Louise replied. "I'm stuck."

"Can you see any reason for her hateful behavior?" I asked. "I mean, not excuse it, but can you understand it at all?"

"No," Louise said. "There was no reason for it. She had everything. Looks, brains, a great husband, money. And my sisters and I were good children. There was no reason for the way she treated us at all."

"Do you think it's possible to forgive someone who did

something bad to you for no reason at all?" I asked.

"Sure. But not if it's something big, and certainly not if it's your whole upbringing and it's your mother who did it."

"But Louise," I said, being dumb again, "you want to be free of her. Soon she will die. You don't want to remain her psychological prisoner even after her death."

"If you're asking me to forgive her, forget it!" she snapped.

"I'm not asking you to forgive her, or to do anything for that matter. I'm just thinking out loud. By the way, *she's* never asked you to forgive her, has she?"

Louise grunted. "Only about a hundred times. Or maybe a thousand. But it's always in these melodramatic scenes, where she is playing the long-suffering mother of an ungrateful daughter. 'Whatever I did wrong when you were a little girl, please forgive me, honey,' she will say. Or, 'I know I must have hurt you, I know I made mistakes, but can't we leave them behind us and move on?' She is so manipulative. She wants a free ride. She wants to pretend that she didn't do what she did. The one thing she wants from me I won't give her, and that's forgiveness. I won't let her go to her grave in peace, so help me I won't, because what she did won't let me live a day on this Earth in peace."

I thought now it was a good time to ask what I hadn't asked, so I did. "What in fact did she do to you? It must have been awful."

"Awful?" Louise paused, as if to look at the word in mid-air. Having inspected it, she gave an ironic smile. "'Awful' is the kind of word someone would use who didn't actually live through my childhood, as I did. I would use a word more like 'artful' or 'calculated.' Among us three children, I was her favorite target, because she knew I knew. She knew I knew what she was up to. She knew I knew she was doing it on purpose. She was able to fool the others into believing it was due to her drinking, or her mental illness, or her not getting enough sleep the night before, or her being under so much pressure, or because Daddy was away. But I knew—and she knew I knew—that none of those was true. She tormented us, and tormented me in particular, for no deeper reason than that she enjoyed it. Some people like tennis, some like bridge, while others like torturing their children. She watered and nurtured my hatred for her as if it were her favorite rose. Her black rose. I told her that in a letter I wrote to her when I was in high school. I told her my love for her grew like a rose, only this rose was black, just as she had raised it to be."

Louise's words, so full of hurt, were not the words of a crazy woman, not by any means. I would learn in future sessions that Louise was the founder and chairperson of a highly successful investment firm outside Boston. She liked her work and she did it well. From all that she told me, she seemed happily married and a good mother of two teens, one in college, one in high school.

But her mother was dying, and she couldn't—or wouldn't—forgive her. She sensed that this was not a good state to be in, so she had come to see me. But what could I do? Could I—should I—prescribe forgiveness? Or a medication? Was there anything useful I could do before her mother died? And who knew how soon that would be?

In my line of work—psychiatry—you have to take into account your own experience and feelings, as well as your patient's. A watch repairman need not worry about his own watch as he works on yours, but a psychiatrist really must listen to his own heart as he works on yours. If I were to help Louise, I needed to listen to what her story brought forth in me.

My own mother was alcoholic. She divorced twice, and she was not able to care for me the way a "good" mother should. She was often drunk when I needed her help. Because of her drinking, she never came to games or school affairs, and she rarely gave me the guidance that I needed. Still, I loved her deeply and hoped every day that she might find happiness in life. She was, in spite of all that she had to contend with, an optimistic person, always looking on the bright side, even when there didn't seem to be one.

There were times when I hated my mother—especially when I was a teen, and she would turn to me in a hugely needy way, asking me to spend time with her, to understand her, to listen to all her woes, to take care of her. I wanted to grow up and be on my way. She wanted me to stay, but I had to push her away, to go to medical school, to make a life for myself. As much as I loved her, I pushed her away, but not without some hatred for myself for doing it—and some hatred for her for setting it all up like this.

But once I got away, forgiving her wasn't hard. I could see her for the vulnerable, loving woman that she was, a woman who had bad luck with men and bad luck inheriting the alcohol gene. I could also see her gloriously good side, her enormous optimism and hopeful soul, as well as her impeccably good taste and good humor, and—when sober—her Audrey Hepburn–like dignity. Had she been born a generation or two later, when women could seek careers more easily, she would have made a great doctor, but she was stuck in her role as a pretty, helpless female, a role that both defined and restrained her all her life.

Gradually, what had been my bad feelings toward her, if not hateful ones, turned to forgiving feelings, and finally grateful and admiring ones. She gave birth to me. She gave me life. She gave me hope. Most importantly, she gave me all she could, and she kept up her hopes as she lived a very difficult, even tragic life. Now I remember my mother with enormous love and respect.

How was my experience with my mother to help me help Louise? Certainly, I had to remind myself that Louise's mother and my mother were two entirely different people, as were Louise and I. But, acknowledging that, was there something in my experience with my mother that could be helpful in Louise's situation?

I thought there was. First of all, what I lived through with my mother helped me empathize with Louise. Although we had different experiences, we both learned too young about how it feels to see the main person in your life—your mother—be out of control, unavailable, disappointing, even hurtful.

Second, my own experience helped me not to judge either Louise or her mother. It helped not to see the issue as one of good versus evil or good guys versus bad guys, but one of life entwined with life.

My job, as I saw it, was not to prescribe forgiveness or medication, but to join Louise and be there as she struggled with her feelings. We would see where they would lead us.

They led us into several years of psychotherapy. Her mother died a few months after our first meeting. I had taken the chance of urging Louise to spend some time talking with her mother before she died. I knew it was not my place to dictate what Louise should do, but at the same time, I had the strong feeling that I would be doing her a disservice if I let her mother die without at least encouraging Louise to try to spend some time with her.

By Louise's account at the time, the meetings with her mother were "predictably worthless and excruciatingly painful." She was angry at me for suggesting that she do it.

However, as the months rolled by, Louise changed how she felt. She was glad she spent those painful moments with her mother before she died. She was glad she had tried. "We didn't get anywhere, in that Mother never changed. But we did get somewhere in that I felt some peace within myself because I had done my best. If I hadn't tried I would have felt that I should have. Having tried, I definitely do not feel that I shouldn't have. So, it was the right thing to do."

Louise never completely forgave her mother. Her anger persisted, and as far as I know, persists to this day. But it is much less than when she came to see me, and it bothers her far less than it used to. Forgiveness is rarely an on/off switch. It operates more on a rheostat.

In one of her last sessions Louise summed up her feelings for what we had done. "When I came to see you, I was sure it was going to be a waste of time. But, still, I came anyway. Whatever it was that brought me to you, against my so-called better judgment, well, I am grateful to that part of me. I am as proud and stubborn as my mother. One of us had to give to get anywhere. I am glad I was the one who gave."

Efforts to make up so often go this way. They happen in

spite of our conscious selves, against our "so-called better judgment," and in a way that can surprise everyone involved. As Louise related to me, "Mother told me she was 'quite surprised' I was coming to see her. She was pleased, but 'quite surprised.' Even that turn of phrase, 'quite surprised,' gave her a tone of moral superiority, as if she were judging me from upon her exalted throne. But that was all right. I could swallow her being quite surprised, because I knew down deep she was totally amazed and ga-ga grateful. She couldn't tell me that, but I knew it."

This is also so often how it goes. One person feigns mild indifference as the other does all the emotional work. But the one who is pretending is weeping tears of joy inside, wishing he or she could summon up the courage to join in more fully.

"You did your best," I said to Louise.

"I always did, with her," came her reply. "Why wasn't it ever good enough?"

"It always was," I said. "She just couldn't tell you so."

"That's not much consolation," Louise said.

"I know, I know," was the best I could reply. But I also knew that Louise was better off now.

Question: I want to reconnect with a former friend, but we did not part on the best of terms. What's the best way to communicate with her? Is e-mail too impersonal?

Answer: You are really asking, "How do I approach someone who I fear may not want to hear from me?" The answer is: slowly.

What's going on now in your relationship? You have not seen each other, she is a "former" friend, but still, something is going on, at least within you, and probably within her. What's going on? You want to see her, so something positive is going on. But you also feel skittish, enough so that you haven't just picked up the telephone and given her a call. In days gone by, you might be considering dispatching a messenger to her with a handwritten note and a bouquet of roses. But it is today, and you are wondering about e-mail.

It doesn't really matter if the message arrives by e-mail or post or carrier pigeon (although that last approach might convey a creativity she'd find refreshing—or an ostentatiousness she'd find annoying). What matters is that the message be brief and honest.

The goal of the message should be to open the door to the next meeting, a face-to-face meeting. Forgiveness—or the working out of any complex set of emotions—is done much better in person than by any other method. Telephone, e-mail, voice mail, posted mail, conference call, video, fax or even carrier pigeon all pale as tools of emotional communication next to what I call the human moment, or face-to-face communication. Your goal should be to sit down with her and talk.

So, send her a brief message, by whatever means you like. Keep it short; don't try to resolve all the issues in the message. Make it honest; don't come off sounding like some slick salesperson. And make it empathic; in other words, try to imagine what she will feel when she gets the note and express your respect for those feelings.

# 13

# What to Do When
# Forgiveness Just Won't Come

**W**hen we forgive, we let someone off the hook, as the saying goes. But what exactly is this hook? It is a psychological hook. The idiom itself gives a wonderful clue as to how to forgive. To forgive, we need to get ourselves off the hook, as much as let the other person off. But, like the hook stuck in the fish's mouth, the hook that sticks in our psyche can be stubborn.

To forgive, we need to spit out the hook. When we can't forgive, we are as hooked as the person we hate. But what if you can't spit out the hook?

A chief motive to forgive, I have suggested, is the realization that you and the world will be better off if you can forgive. The part of forgiveness that feels good and conveys the health benefits associated with forgiveness is renouncing the anger and resentment you feel whenever you think of the person who betrayed you or hurt you or humiliated you—or did whatever he or she did to make you feel so angry and resentful. It is hard to come by.

For example, you may feel happily dispose

forgiveness in the abstract, but when the image of your enemy—your ex, the boss who fired you, the person who sued you, the terrorist who killed your son—comes to mind, your stomach fills with acid and your mind fills with rage. The automatic, physiological response feels out of your control. How can you eradicate that?

It helps, first, to look for the hook.

When we can't forgive, the hook keeps digging into us as we keep feeling the pangs of anger and resentment toward the other person. We keep wishing them ill, imagining their demise or simply tearing them down in our inner monologue, all the while overlooking that our anger is driving the hook deeper and deeper not into them, but into us.

This psychological hook can be sharper and more stubborn than any metal one. Think how hooked Captain Ahab was. Or Hamlet. Or Othello. Each of them was hooked by a massive desire for revenge that finally led to their own tragic deaths.

I've been hooked, haven't you? Not as grandly or as tragically as Captain Ahab or the other great figures from literature, but hooked nonetheless.

Divorcing and divorced couples do this all the time. People who have been betrayed do this. Almost anytime someone you once liked or loved does you wrong, you do this. You just do not want to say good-bye and leave it at that. You want your pound of flesh. Staying hooked is also a way of maintaining contact with someone you once cared for deeply.

But what if you do not know the person? If a total stranger mugs you in the street and steals your money, you feel angry. If you continue to feel angry, it is not because you are sad that you can't be friends with the mugger anymore. After all, he was a total stranger. But you do feel a hidden sadness nonetheless.

You feel sad that you got mugged. You feel sad that a horrible thing happened. You feel sad that life rose up and swatted you. You feel sad that you couldn't repel the mugger. You might even feel sad about the presence of muggers out there in the world. And, if you are really sensitive, you might feel sad that this mugger couldn't think of any better way to live his life than to attack people on the street.

But such sadness makes you feel nervous and vulnerable, so you cover it over with anger and resentment. The anger makes total sense. But, if you are still feeling it a year later, then probably, at least in part, you have not allowed yourself to feel sad over what happened. Instead you feel only anger, even hatred.

A teacher of mine once told me, "The opposite of love is not hatred. The opposite of love is indifference." Hatred keeps us involved with a person, an event, a group, something from the past, whatever it might be. Where there is hatred, there is involvement and connection. If you keep on hating the mugger—or the killer, the batterer or whomever—you stay involved. Sometimes you may choose to do this, feeling that such involvement is useful, as in continuing to hate the Nazis. But most of the time continued hating is a bad idea that does not serve you well. A better approach is to let go of your involvement with the mugger.

You will help yourself let him go if you let yourself feel sad, not just angry, about what happened. You will help yourself if you let yourself know that you cannot change the past by being angry about it.

For example, I once had a close friend named Luke who one day received a huge promotion and became immensely influential in his field. From that day on, he treated me like a person who was beneath him. If I called him, he had his secretary speak to me. He still maintained the appearance of friendship with me, in that he invited me to parties and was civil when we spoke, but he had his secretary call me with the invitation and at parties he would look past me as we spoke. I wasn't influential enough to matter to him anymore. Naturally, my feelings were hurt, and I was angry with my friend. When I told him so, he laughed and said I was imagining things. I knew I wasn't, but I also found out that he was not going to talk about it honestly with me.

I was hooked by my anger for this man. I couldn't shake the hook. It just dug deeper and deeper into me.

Whenever I thought of him I would mutter to myself about what a jerk he was. Whenever I got a message from him (or his secretary), I bristled. Even as we grew distant, I still felt anger and resentment whenever he came to mind. The hook had stuck.

I was hooked because I was sad, but hadn't let myself face how sad I felt. I missed Luke. We had been friends, and I missed seeing him. When he changed—and, as we all know, some people do change for the worse when they become famous—I couldn't get angry, then let the anger go, because I couldn't accept my sadness over the fact that we would not be friends anymore. By remaining angry, I held on to my hope that Luke might change back to the good guy he used to be.

I was stuck in a spot of, if not hating Luke, then at least

feeling ongoing anger and resentment toward him because I didn't want to lose him altogether. Anger was the hook within me whose barb I needed to flatten.

The way to do that was to accept what had happened and to grieve. I had to feel my sadness over my loss of my friend. The old Luke had died. I had to accept that, feel sad, say good-bye and move on. Forgiving is a kind of mourning, a giving up on certain hopes.

But the job was not complete just in mourning the loss of the Luke I had known and cared for so much. It still rankled me that he had succumbed to such vanity. How could he do that? And why did I care so much?

I cared so much because I felt competitive. This was another barb, another key to my forgiving Luke: seeing a part of myself that I didn't want to see. I was envious of the power and prestige Luke had acquired. Even though I did not want his job, I was envious of the perks that came with it. Envy is another form of anger.

The best cure for anger is, first of all, time; second is empathy. You have to allow yourself to feel the first burst of anger. Someone rejects you. You feel angry. Someone insults you. You feel angry. Someone is late. You feel angry. The short-term response of anger is as normal and inevitable as your stomach growling when you swallow air.

But the longer-term response is what I needed to work on with Luke. I was still feeling envious and angry long after those feelings should have abated. This is where empathy became key. Empathy for Luke, but also empathy for myself.

In order to defuse the anger prompted by the question, *How could he do that?* I needed to empathize with Luke. But in order to defuse the anger prompted by the question, *Why do I care?* I needed to empathize with myself.

By empathize, I mean understand someone's actions in a context that makes sympathetic sense of those actions, as opposed to merely judging the person or seeing no other motivation than motiveless malignity or evil.

When I thought about it, I could see other reasons that Luke could have changed than just his becoming a jerk. The power of his new position was a stronger drug than he could handle. I didn't have to be a psychiatrist to understand that Luke, who had grown up under the thumb of a highly successful and domineering father, craved power for himself. When he finally found it, it made him a bit crazy. Understanding how his response related to issues from his growing up helped me let go of my resentment toward Luke because I could see his actions in understandable, forgivable terms. Once I could understand his preening and boasting in human terms and place them in a life story I could make sense of, then I felt much less anger or resentment. As the old saying goes, "To understand all is to forgive all."

The same process helped me with the question, *Why did I care?* Losing Luke as a friend made me sad. That made sense. All loss leads to sadness, and the best response is to grieve, which means to feel the sadness, talk about it, cry over it, until it gradually becomes a part of our hard-won store of personal wisdom. But why did I take my feelings to the next step and feel diminished myself by Luke's sudden surge of success? Why did I feel reduced in the eyes of the world, simply because Luke had soared so high?

At this point, I needed to empathize with myself. Instead of feeling angry or ashamed toward myself for having the feelings I had, I needed to remind myself that I had never had the kind of stable childhood most people need in order to feel solid and secure as adults. Indeed, my childhood had been highly unstable. My father had bipolar disorder and was hospitalized several times in state mental hospitals. My mother divorced him and remarried to an abusive alcoholic, as she became alcoholic herself, then divorced my stepfather after seven tumultuous years. My rocky beginning made me insecure as an adult. I needed to empathize with myself and realize that my reactions to Luke's behavior were overreactions brought about by my fundamental sense of insecurity. Losing Luke made me more than sad; it made me panicky, because it brought up old feelings of insecurity from years ago, feelings for which I never developed the psychological armor of protection.

While I couldn't change my insecurity, I could extend a helping hand to myself, so to speak, and not give myself a hard time for having the feelings I had. I could identify their source and realize they came from my past, not from some evil side of Luke that I had to punish or some mean side of me for which I had to feel ashamed.

Two keys to finding the hook, then, are empathizing with yourself and empathizing with the other person. Even if you do not know the other person, you can make up a story about why the person might have done what he or she did.

Question: I'm really angry and hurt that my boyfriend just dumped me. Should I try to fix the relationship or just let it go? What can I do if he rebuffs me?

**Answer:** Your question points up how important it is to acknowledge all that you're feeling before you jump into action. You feel angry and hurt. Okay, stay with that for a moment before you decide what to do next. Let yourself feel the hurt. Why did he dump you? How does being dumped (what a term!) make you feel? Embarrassed? Afraid? Before you say, "Angry!" first acknowledge the more vulnerable feelings of inferiority, embarrassment and fear.

As you feel those, you might ask yourself, *Was my boyfriend helping me grow stronger, or was he my shield against my underlying feelings of inferiority, embarrassment and fear in life in general? Did his dumping me make me look at who I really am? Should I work on that, before I swing into action trying to get my boyfriend back, or getting all worked up into a rage at him?*

When you ask, "What can I do if he rebuffs me?" my reply is, "Be stronger next time." In other words, I think you should take this moment of being dumped as an opportunity to get to work on yourself.

"What do you mean, 'work on myself'?" you might ask.

I mean to work on strengthening the healthy connections that you already have: connections with your family, friends, groups and organizations you care about, and even your pet, or with activities you like, from sports to listening to music to working out. Work on your connection with your physical body; try to get yourself to a place where you feel good about how you look.

If your boyfriend dumped you, as you say, he should try to get you back, not vice versa. In the meantime, take as a call to action the feelings that being dumped exposed in you. Make yourself a stronger woman.

Forgiveness is not called for here. Strengthening yourself and your life is.

# 14

# A Family Feud

**M**y own family has taught me how difficult forgiveness can be.

As I mentioned earlier, my father and his brother, my Uncle Jim, waged a pointless, bitter feud with each other for the last several decades of their lives. When my father died, the feud had not been resolved. When my uncle died some ten years later, his feelings about my father had not changed. The two of them never forgave each other, and they never reconciled. That's one reason I am writing this book—in the hope that you can help your father and uncle, or others you care for, to reconcile before they die, or that you can help yourself to forgive or seek forgiveness now, before your life ends.

As is so often the case in feuds, it was never clear what my father and uncle wanted each other to own up to or apologize for having done. All I know is that nasty words spewed forth, harsh judgments froze previously warm feelings, everybody looked for cover and took sides, while an unbridgeable distance grew between two brothers who had grown up as the best of friends.

It was all so sad and unnecessary. As kids, Dad and Uncle Jim were champion sailors on Cape Cod, sailing out of Hyannis, Wiano, Osterville, and anywhere else there was a good race. Between the two of them, they won dozens of trophies. They could team up in a boat like no other tandem. Dad was great at getting to the starting line just as the gun went off, and Uncle Jim was great at anticipating the moves of other boats in order to get the best of the wind. As a racing team, they were all but unbeatable.

But they were both strange birds in their own way.

My father was a star athlete at Harvard, class of 1936, an All-American in hockey and a dashing young man, or so I am told. Not long after my father married my mother, he went off to war and became the captain of a destroyer escort. Fighting submarines took a terrible toll on him. When he came back from the war, he went crazy and was committed to a mental hospital, or what I grew up calling an insane asylum.

Dad was diagnosed schizophrenic and received multiple rounds of electric shock treatment as well as insulin shock treatment. Years later he told me how he dreaded the insulin shock the most because it gave him the terrifying feeling that he was falling uncontrollably.

Then a young psychiatrist rethought my father's diagnosis and put him on what was then a radical new medication called Lithium. It worked a miracle. Dad got better, left the hospital and spent the last twenty years of his life teaching public school in Derry, New Hampshire. However, the family had been broken while my father was crazy; my mother divorced him when I was four.

My Uncle Jim, who was four years older than my father,

also went to Harvard. He was short—about five feet six—and was tough, excelling as a boxer. He was also brilliant. He majored in both physics and Romance languages. His only problem was that he didn't know how to fit into life. When he married my aunt, she hoped he would go into the world of Boston finance. But underneath this boxer's tough exterior, Uncle Jim was afraid. Even though he was smarter than just about anybody, and physically tough, he had no confidence in himself.

Turning away from business, Uncle Jim took my aunt and went farming in Pepperell, Massachusetts. They had two children, who were like siblings to me. One of them, Josselyn, died at the age of fifty-six. I told her story elsewhere in this book. The other, Jamie, is my dear and close friend and brother.

While Dad was in the war, Uncle Jim worked the farm. After the war ended, I was born, the third of three boys. By the time of the divorce, Uncle Jim had sold his farm and moved to Chatham, on Cape Cod, where he opened a candle-pin bowling alley.

The feud began after my grandmother—my father and uncle's mother—died. Gammy Hallowell, as I called her, had held us all together, somehow ruling over the differences between her sons, and hosting the glorious Thanksgivings I remember so well, even after the divorce. Gammy managed to keep peace.

But once she died, the schism opened, never again to close. It started over a dispute about the inheritance. The conflict focused on one item. My grandmother owned an antique silver tea service that had been in the family for many years.

Upon Gammy's death, it was supposed to go to Josselyn. However, my father contested this point, or so I was told. From then on, for all the years between my grandmother's death and my father's death, that silver separated the brothers—and other members of the family—a glistening symbol of what can go wrong between people who love each other.

What kept this feud alive is what keeps all such feuds alive: people's pigheadedness. If anyone was right, I don't know who that was. I don't even know the truth of what happened. I heard two unreliable versions: my father's and Uncle Jim's. Then I heard various relatives' versions. Based on that mishmash, I was supposed to make up my own mind.

I couldn't. When the feud started I was sixteen. From the beginning, I didn't know what to make of it. All I knew was that the situation made me sad. I wished the arguing and side-taking would end.

I wanted the two sides to make up. I wanted us to have Thanksgiving dinner together, the big, happy kind we used to have when I was a little boy, before the feud.

But what I wanted never happened. Each of us five grandchildren made various attempts to reconcile the two sides. Each of our attempts only made matters worse. Someone would feel betrayed by the person who was trying to make peace. We all discovered that it was much safer to stay out of the conflict, or to pick one side, swear our allegiance and never stray.

If we tried to see the point of view of the other side, those aligned with that side would call us disloyal, uninformed or merely naive. Dad thought he was totally right. Uncle Jim thought he was totally right. Uncle Jim thought Dad was crazy, and he had a psychiatric diagnosis to back up his opinion. Dad thought Uncle Jim was a liar, and he could cite evidence to back up his version of things.

The debates grew predictable and monotonous, but still painful, marring holidays, birthdays, family get-togethers and everybody's feelings of joy.

I always wondered, *Why didn't they just go out for a sail together and make up? Why didn't they find a way to forgive?*

I *was* naive, I guess. When you look at the history of families, not to mention the history of the world, you see how rarely people go out for a sail together and make up.

But isn't it sad? My family gave up all those happy Thanksgivings we could have had together before people started to die, all those happy birthdays, all those pleasant letters (and later e-mails), all those daily doses of love and security and respect we could have felt from each other, and we exchanged them—for what? For my point of view over yours. We exchanged them for a pointless, stupid feud.

What would it have taken for Uncle Jim to call my father one day and say, "Let's talk." Or what would it have taken for my father to call Uncle Jim one day and say, "Let's move on." Whatever it would have taken, it never took. It never even came close.

I loved them both. I loved Uncle Jim as if he were my father, and indeed, I spent more time with him than Dad because of the divorce. But I also loved Dad, my father, as much as I loved Uncle Jim.

That's what made it so hard to take sides, or to listen in silence when in my presence one of them was criticized by someone else. I would think to myself, *Why can't they just make up? Why can't we stop all this?* I would resolve to find a way to bring these two wonderful men back together. But I never did. No one did.

There was no bad guy. My uncle and father were both good guys, very good guys, whom I deeply loved and still do. That they never could forgive was one of the greatest sadnesses of their lives, and of the entire family's as well. Hatred within families may be the most damaging and enduring of all human conflicts, and the most difficult to sort out.

If such a feud is tearing your family apart, I urge you to seek help from outside your family. Family therapy has made great progress in the last twenty-five years. Most clinical social workers are trained in it, and their fees are not high.

Attempts to resolve these feuds from the inside run the risk of making matters worse, as happened in my family. You might succeed, but if you try and fail, don't give up. People are going to die. It is better to make some kind of peace before that happens. Finding a good family therapist and investing in some serious family work can bring resolution to the grimmest of family conflicts.

Question: My sister and I have recently forgiven each other for years of accumulated hurts and mis-understandings. What can I do to ensure that our differences no longer truly stand in the way of maintaining a relationship?

Answer: This question points up an important fact not only about forgiveness but about human nature itself. Our feelings change every day. You might have forgiven each other on Tuesday, but come Friday the old doubts may start to creep back in, so that by the following Tuesday you feel as resentful as ever.

Another way of putting it is to say that relationships are like roofs. They can spring a leak at any time, and they must be worked on to be kept in good repair. With this recent forgiveness, you got a new roof, but you have to keep it in good repair. Roofs, like relationships, suffer if they are neglected.

The antidote is regular contact. Also, give each other permission to be honest. Acknowledge the fact that all relationships are ambivalent. Most of us don't feel 100 percent positive about anybody, even ourselves. Just because you have forgiven each other after years of hurt, don't expect yourselves suddenly to love each other completely.

What you can start to do, now that you have forgiven one another, is enjoy the company of each other once again. Enjoying someone's company over the long term includes being able to be angry at them now and then.

As long as you work at maintaining contact and keeping the relationship in a good state of repair, you will have the great pleasure of a strong and true relationship with your sister.

# 15

# Beware of What's Called Justice

*ustice* is a deceptive word. Often, it merely means
revenge.

We have a system of laws to enforce our codes of justice,
a system that we certainly need. I do not quarrel with that.
My point here is not political but psychological. The bright,
shining shield called justice can blind us, and it often has.

My uncle and my father feuded until they died. Both were
convinced justice was on their side. Both spent hundreds of
hours, I am sure, marshalling evidence in their minds of the
other's wrongdoing. Both felt morally superior in their
respective positions, and both could have put on a brilliant
case in court.

But they didn't really want justice. They wanted to prove
the other wrong. They wanted to win the fight. They each
wanted the other to apologize.

What got lost in this fight for "justice" was what mattered
the most: love between two brothers and harmony in an
extended family.

When I see an adult demanding justice, nostrils flaring and

cheeks on fire, I think of my seven-year-old son demanding justice, as he wails that it is unfair and unjust for his mother and me to demand that he brush his teeth every morning and every evening. They are his teeth, and he should be able to do with them what he wants! Beware of the word "justice" outside of a courtroom. It is a cover for many less noble words, such as vengeance, selfishness, pride, fear and prejudice. When someone says, "All I want is justice," I think of my son, trying to get out of brushing his teeth, or I think of a lynch mob, ruled by fear and a primitive desire to act rather than reflect.

The great irony is that the demand for justice often leads to gross injustice. I don't quarrel that we need judges and punishments in the service of justice. I am just terribly wary of which humans are qualified to sit in judgment or mete out punishments.

When I see how hideously the idea of justice can get twisted—when I envision those planes flying into the World Trade Center in the name of what their pilots called justice, or when I think of the Great Inquisition, or imagine "witches" being burned alive and epileptics condemned to death because of purported satanic possession—I cringe at how incompetent we humans have proven ourselves to be, time and time again, in determining what is just.

And yet "justice" remains one of the most common reasons people can't or won't try to forgive.

But we'd all be doomed if justice were meted out everywhere it was due. As Shakespeare wrote in *The Merchant of Venice:*

*Though justice be thy plea, consider this,*
*That in the course of justice, none of us*
*Should see salvation: we do pray for mercy,*
*And that same prayer doth teach us all to render*
*The deeds of mercy.*

Or, as a prayer asks, "Forgive us our trespasses, *as we for-*
*give those who trespass against us. . . .*" As much as we might
want to even the score, we all will need forgiveness and mercy
before our time is up on this Earth—not to mention afterwards!
On the journey to justice, we each meet ourselves walking the
other way. Just as I might think of throttling the woman who
cut in line and took her Mountain Dew before me, I need to
remind myself of the many times I have acted or spoken in
far more wicked ways than that woman did on that day.

The French philosopher Montaigne put it like this, some
five hundred years ago: "There is no man so good that if he
placed all his actions and thoughts under the scrutiny of the
laws, he would not deserve hanging ten times in his life."

The wise among us know this. We were taught it in school.
We have discovered it in life, but in the heat of the moment
we all forget it.

I try to teach myself that I am as flawed as the man driving the BMW that I attacked. Indeed, I have behaved much
worse than the woman who cut me off in line; when I reflect
upon it, I know that it is true. I have. Then I hope for mercy.

How quickly I change from being the self-righteous man
whose spot in the cold-drink line has been taken to a fearful
man in need of mercy when I am stopped by a traffic cop—or
worse, when I am stopped by the memory of some bad thing
I did years ago.

I have to remind myself that I have cut in line and stolen parking spots and done much, much worse than that many, many times. I have to remind myself that if I were to receive justice, that justice would do me in. I need mercy and forgiveness much more. When I consider all that I have done wrong, I become more forgiving toward others.

The most famous story illustrating this idea comes from the Gospel of John in the New Testament. It is such a short story that I quote it here in its entirety, as taken from the New Revised Standard Version.

Early in the morning he came again to the temple. All the people came to him and he sat down and began to teach them. The scribes and the Pharisees brought a woman who had been caught in adultery; and making her stand before all of them, they said to him, "Teacher, this woman was caught in the very act of committing adultery. Now in the law Moses commanded us to stone such women. Now what do you say?" They said this to test him, so they might have some charge to bring against him. Jesus bent down and wrote with his finger on the ground. When they kept on questioning him, he straightened up and said to them, "Let anyone among you who is without sin be the first to throw a stone at her." And once again he bent down and wrote on the ground. When they heard it, they went away, one by one, beginning with the elders; and Jesus was left alone with the woman standing before him. Jesus straightened up and said to her, "Woman, where are they? Has no one condemned you?" She said, "No one, sir." And Jesus said, "Neither do I condemn you. Go your way, and from now on do not sin again." (John 8:2–11)

Of course, our penal system can't instruct all judges to say to convicted criminals, "Go your way, and from now on, do not sin again." But then again, none of our judges is Jesus.

The practical point of this story, and Shakespeare's words, and Montaigne's—all from differing cultures—is that when it comes to demanding justice we had each better be careful. The righteous indignation of the mob is like a drug; it makes us drunk with a desire to condemn and to punish.

Before any of us judges anyone else, we should pause.

We have a legal system to do that. But before we augment that delicate system by joining the mob, before we harden our hearts and carry on vendettas and feuds, putting our correct point of view above the other person's incorrect point of view, we should consider looking away from the mob, stooping down and writing in the sand. We should consider looking at our own wrongs and our own lives.

This is where forgiveness starts: in the honest searching of our own hearts.

*The Master and the student are sitting by the side of the road together, contemplating life and eating brown rice from wooden bowls.*

*"I hate this stuff," the Master says, spitting some rice on the ground. "Isn't there a Burger King down that way?"*

*"But Master," the student protests, "Burger King unbalances your fatty acids and cholesterol."*

*"Do you know what a pain in the butt you are?" the Master asks. "Why don't you just live a little and stop denying yourself everything in the name of finding some magical mental state?"*

*"But that is why I am studying with you," the student says. "You are a supreme guide to enlightenment."*

*"Where did you hear that?" the Master asks.*

*"Everyone knows it," the student says and falls silent, sensing that the Master is taunting him once again.*

*The two of them sit in silence for a while, munching on their brown rice.*

*Suddenly the Master throws his arms around the student and proclaims, "I love you! You are my best student ever."*

*The student feels overcome with emotion. He searches for the right response, but can only say, "Thank you, Master. I feel very humble."*

*They sit in silence for quite a while. They finish their rice, and they fold their hands and they focus on their breathing.*

*"I didn't mean it," the Master says at the end of a long breath.*

*"You didn't mean what?" the student asks, knowing all too well what is coming.*

*"I don't love you. And you are not my best student ever."*

*The student sits in silence, trying not to weep. He feels crushed. More time passes as he tries to compose a response. Finally he asks, "Then why did you tell me that you loved me and that I was your best student ever?"*

*"I meant it when I said it," the Master replies. "And then,*

*when I said I didn't mean it, I meant that, too."*

*"So I should never believe what you say?"* the student asks.

*"No, quite the opposite,"* the Master replies. *"You should believe everything I say. However, you should not expect what I say to be the same from moment to moment or from day to day."*

*"Then I can't depend upon you?"* the student asks.

*"You can depend upon me to be as undependable as everything else in life,"* the Master says. *They sit in silence. Then the Master asks,* *"Do you hate me for telling you that I loved you?"*

*"I want to be honest with you. Yes, I do hate you for telling me that."*

*"And for telling you that you were my best student ever?"*

*"Yes, I hate you especially for telling me that. It was all that I had ever hoped for."*

*"And who is hurt when you hate me?"* the Master asks.

*"I am hurt,"* the student replies.

*"Then you should forgive me,"* the Master replies, *"and move on."*

*"No, I should kill you and then move on, so you cannot hurt any more people,"* the student says.

*"And if you killed me, then how would you feel?"* the Master asks.

*"I would feel proud, as if I had removed a vermin from the face of the Earth,"* the student says, red-faced in anger.

*"You mean that now,"* the Master says, *"just as I meant it when I said that I loved you. Our feelings can be treacherous guides."*

*The student's breathing slows and his face becomes less red.* *"I am tired of all this,"* he says. *"You make life far too complicated."*

*"I know, it is much simpler when all you have to do is judge, kill and move on."*

*"You make me tired," the student says.*

*"You are doing well," the Master replies. "You have stayed put. You have not run away and you have not killed me. Most students try to do one or the other. Rest assured, I am tired, too. Yet we are both still here and alive. We must be working hard."*

*"Why is life so much work?" the student asks.*

*"Because people are so stupid and stubborn," the Master replies.*

*"And what can we do to overcome that?" the student asks.*

*"We can't overcome it," the Master replies. "It is who we are. But we can recognize it and try to stay put, rather than running away or killing the people who anger us."*

*"I wouldn't have killed you," the student says. "I was just angry."*

*"And I wouldn't have loved you," the Master replies. "I was just crazy."*

*The student sits and thinks while the Master wipes his bowl with a red cloth. "You stay here and think," the Master says. "I am going to Burger King."*

# 16

## Forgiving a Betrayer

et me let Henry Davis (I've changed his name, but his
story is true) tell you about an act of forgiveness that
will amaze you.

Henry Davis is one of the world's great experts on forgiveness. I met him when I was in Greensboro, North Carolina, in
the spring of 2001. He was my cab driver on my trip from
Greensboro to Winston-Salem.

Henry and I started talking as we drove along the sunny
North Carolina highway. I could tell right away he came from
one of the fundamentalist Christian traditions, as he made
more references to the Lord in five minutes than most cab
drivers usually do in a year.

He also had the gift of rhetoric. He went on a complicated
riff about the power of God when I asked a few questions. I,
myself, believe in God, but my faith is not as sure as Henry's
is. As he talked, I felt a bit put off, as I usually do when I
encounter fervent belief, caught between feeling amazed,
skeptical and left out.

But the more he talked, the more Henry drew me in. He

really felt all that he said. He was no con man, nor was he one of those salesmen who just likes to hear himself talk. Like many religious people, he was excited by what he took to be eternal truths. However, not only religious people do this. I know physicists who do it, and philosophers, even football fans.

Henry told me all he could, a man sharing something he loved. I soon found out that he had lived a lot of life. He had grown up on a farm in North Carolina, one of twenty-seven children. Yes, that's right. His mother and father raised twenty-seven children. I didn't ask, but I imagine there must have been some multiple births, maybe a few adoptions. Henry told me, "Daddy made us work the farm. If we got out of line, he'd knock us down, so we didn't get out of line very often. We were poor, but we never wanted for anything we needed."

Henry wanted to leave the farm. So, when he got old enough, he set out for New York, where he became a member of the New York City Police Department. Everything went smoothly for a while as he moved up the ranks.

One day he received an assignment that changed his life forever. Along with two other officers, he was given the duty of transferring a member of an organized crime group from one lock-up to another. Henry and the two other officers took the prisoner in handcuffs and leg-irons to an armored transport vehicle. Henry drove. Halfway to their destination, shots rang out. The other officers got out of the truck, while Henry stayed inside to guard the prisoner. He saw his two fellow officers get hit just before he felt a sharp pain in his back and lost consciousness. He remembers nothing more.

Henry's superior officer had accepted an $850,000 bribe to

reveal the route the prisoner would take. The two officers accompanying Henry were killed. Henry survived, but he was paralyzed from the waist down.

Over the next two years he worked relentlessly in physical therapy under the supervision of a skilled and inspiring nurse. Miraculously, contrary to what all the doctors had told him, he regained full use of his legs. When he left his wheelchair, he asked the nurse who had helped him with his physical therapy to marry him. She accepted. She was still his wife when I met Henry that day in the cab.

I asked Henry what had become of the officer who had betrayed him. "He's doing time," Henry told me. "He'll be in jail for a long while."

"Have you seen him since you were shot?" I asked.

"Oh, yes," Henry immediately replied. "I went to visit him pretty soon after he got to the prison. I had to let him know that I forgave him. I told him that whatever forgiveness he needed now, it would come from God, because I had forgiven him completely and honestly. I told him I understood that Satan had got a hold of his mind, that greed had taken over, and that under the influence of greed he had done something that he never, ever would have done had Satan not won the battle for his soul right then.

"He started to cry and asked how I could forgive him for having done what he had done. I told him my part was easy. It wasn't going to help me any to hate him. All that hating would do would be to corrupt my own soul and make my life worse, so I forgave him because it was the best thing for me to do. He couldn't believe it. I told him over and over again that I bore him no ill will. I told him I forgave him, and I prayed he would find forgiveness from God.

"He told me he didn't believe in God. I told him that didn't matter. He should just open his heart in prayer and God would find him and grant him forgiveness. He said he didn't know how to do that. I told him he would learn, if he tried. And that was the last I saw of him. I might go back and see how he's doing one of these days."

"But Henry," I said, "he tried to have you killed. You were left paralyzed. How could you forgive him?"

"All you have to do is open your heart to the power of love and you can forgive anyone," Henry replied. "How could I not forgive him, if God forgave us for killing his only son?"

"You make it sound so simple," I said. "But if someone had done to me what he did to you, I don't know if I could forgive him."

"What earthly good would it do you to keep hating him?" Henry asked. "It would just make you sick inside, and it would separate you from God."

"I wouldn't be able to control it," I said. "I wouldn't keep hating him because I wanted to keep hating him. The hatred would just live on whether I wanted it to or not. Every time I thought of what he had done to me, my hatred would rise up, no matter how much I tried to will it not to."

"Well, let me ask you a question," Henry said, as we kept motoring down the North Carolina roads. "You have children?"

"Yes," I said. "Three of them. They're eleven, eight and five. Pretty small family compared to what you grew up with."

"No doubt," Henry said. "But tell me, does one of your kids

ever say he hates his brother because his brother stole his sneakers or something like that?"

"Oh, yes," I replied.

"And what do you say? Do you say, well, go right ahead and hate him because what he did was wrong?"

"No, I try to intervene and get them to talk and to make up."

"And does that always work?"

"No," I said with a chuckle, "it does not."

"And then what do you do?" Henry asked me. "Do you give up on them as hateful devils and turn your attention somewhere else? Of course you don't. You may get impatient or angry with them, but you still try to teach them how to share and how to forgive and how to love each other, even though they don't necessarily learn very well. You do that, don't you?" Henry asked, looking at me through the rear-view mirror, the whites of his eyes a sharp contrast to the dark pupils.

"I try to," I said.

"Of course you do. And that is what God is doing with us. We are all God's children, and we can't get along. But God doesn't walk away from us. So we surely shouldn't walk away from each other."

*Okay,* I thought to myself, *I'll just keep asking him the bald, flat-footed questions that I wrestle with. He's got answers.* "But Henry," I went on, "doesn't it turn you into a doormat if you keep forgiving people? I mean, aren't you setting yourself up to get taken advantage of? If you keep turning the other cheek, you're going to get beat up, don't you think?"

"We all get beat up in this life," Henry immediately replied. "It's just a matter of what cause do you want to get beat up for. I'd rather get beat up in the name of love and forgiveness than in the name of vengeance."

"But don't you think you should defend yourself?" I asked.

Henry whistled. "Of course you should. That night, I tried to defend myself. I didn't say, 'Here I am, brother, shoot me.' But once it was over, the only way for me to make it truly be over and to square myself with what I believe in was to forgive that man. Since I had been practicing how to do that just about every day of my life, it wasn't all that hard."

"What if you'd killed him defending yourself?" I asked.

"If I could have killed him, I would have. I am far from perfect. But, if I had killed him before he shot me, I never would have been paralyzed, which means I never would have met the love of my life."

"Are you saying you're glad it happened?" I asked.

"Of course not, my man! I'm not crazy. But I am saying that we can't always pick and choose what's gonna happen to us. We gotta be ready to take what comes and make the best out of it."

I paused, thinking about something he had said. "You said a minute ago that you have been practicing how to forgive the man who betrayed you every day of your life. What did you mean by that?"

Henry laughed. "Are you a reporter or something? You do ask a lot of questions. But that's good. It is good to have an inquiring heart."

"No," I said. "I'm not a reporter. But I truly do want to know what you have to say."

"You Christian?" Henry asked.

"Yes," I replied, "just not as Christian as you are."

Henry chuckled. "I asked because if you were brought up a Christian the way I was, you'd know very well what I mean by practicing every day of my life. Ever since I can remember I would kneel by my bed every night and pray for forgiveness for me and my family, and then for all my friends, and then, and this was the hard part, for all my enemies. That's what I mean by practice. Naturally, I would ask my daddy why in the world I was supposed to forgive my enemy. 'It's easy to forgive your friend,' Daddy would say. 'Forgiving your enemy takes guts.' And of course I'd ask him the same kind of questions you been asking me. And he'd answer sort of like I been answering you. It's the only way that makes sense. You can see that, can't you?"

"I can see that it makes sense. But I'm not sure I can see how to do it. And a lot of people who were brought up Christian like you don't forgive much either."

"Ain't that the truth?" Henry agreed. "I'm not saying you have to be brought up like me. I just say you need some instruction from somewhere about Satan and how to resist him and his temptations. And taking vengeance in your own hands is a mighty powerful temptation."

"So how do you do it? How do you resist?" I asked, persisting like an annoying disciple-in-the-making.

"You try with all your heart and all your soul and all your mind. You pray. You commit yourself every day to trying to love your neighbor as yourself. It is the hardest thing you'll ever do, but nothing matters more than doing that. It's what keeps us from being lost souls."

*Maybe he has a key,* I thought to myself, *even for non-Christians.* Keeping hatred alive really would make his life worse. Maybe his Christian explanation is also a highly sophisticated psychological solution.

If you take the words like "God," "Lord," "Satan," and so forth out of what Henry said and replace them with secular words like "goodness" or "evil," his remarks still cohere and make sense. You can even take the words toward a more psychological level and use terms like those George Vaillant, a psychiatrist at Harvard, has used in his long-standing work on the "hierarchy of defenses."

What Vaillant calls the "mature psychological defenses" include suppression, anticipation, altruism and humor. His research, which is empirical and spans decades of his following a large group of individuals over the course of their lives, has found that the people who are the healthiest and happiest resort to the mature defenses in dealing with stress.

When I asked Henry how he was able to resist the temptation to take revenge instead of forgive, he replied in Judeo-Christian terms, "You commit yourself every day to trying to love your neighbor as yourself." In Vaillant's psychological terms, this concept could be restated as, "You commit yourself every day to trying to rely on the defense of altruism."

As we drove on in the cab—Henry was driving me some seventy miles from one place where I was giving a lecture to another—we kept talking. Henry continued to speak with such unsplintered conviction that it was hard for me not to believe he was right. "Do you think that the man who set you up to be ambushed is praying for forgiveness now?" I asked Henry.

"I hope he is. I have forgiven him myself, and the rest has to come from the Lord. If he lets the Lord in, the Lord will come, and he'll be forgiven. That's for sure."

"But how does he let the Lord in if he doesn't believe in the Lord?" I asked, speaking for all of us who are less faithful than Henry.

Henry smacked the steering wheel. "Don't you see? You don't have to believe to feel the presence of God. You might not call it God. When my little grandson jumps up into my arms, God is there, even though my grandson doesn't know much about God. God was here before we were."

"But still, that man in prison is lost in guilt. What can he do?"

"He can do what we all can do," Henry replied. "Open his heart up to the healing power of love."

Question: What's the good of forgiving someone? Won't this just reopen old wounds?

Answer: Just the opposite. Holding a grudge keeps the wound festering. The only way to close it is to heal it, and the best way to do that is to forgive. You'll have to acknowledge some strong and unpleasant feelings, but only if you do that can you start to let them go.

There is no guarantee, sad to say, that even if you do acknowledge the feelings of anger and hurt, you will then be able to forgive. Sometimes the anger and hurt last your whole life long. But if you are able to begin to see the situation from the other person's point of view, just a little bit, you might be able to get past the anger and the hurt to forgiveness. Then you will have done a wonderful thing.

Let me give you an example from my own life that I am still working on. Early in my career, a small group of people turned against me. I needed help from my friends. One friend, in particular, could have helped me a great deal, but he decided to take a neutral position, saying he could see the point of view of the people who were attacking me as well as he could see my point of view. I felt deeply hurt. I felt that a true friend was showing himself to be weak when I needed him most, choosing his own comfort and safety over sticking his neck out for me, his friend.

Many years have passed since then. I haven't forgiven him. We are still friends, but I hold this against him. I can't stop myself. As much as I believe in forgiveness, I can't will myself to forgive. I have followed the steps I know can lead to forgiveness. I have acknowledged my anger and hurt. I have tried to empathize with my friend. I have tried to let go of my resentment, but it hasn't worked yet. I still find myself feeling disappointed in him and resenting him for not standing strong on my behalf. He probably resents me for putting him in this situation. He probably resents me for mistakes I made leading up to the situation. I don't know for sure, because we have never really sat down and talked it through. That is something we should do. It is the only way I will truly and deeply forgive him, and he me.

But it is hard. I am supposedly an expert on forgiveness, but I haven't done it yet. None of us is as expert at forgiving as we could be. The best I can do, the best any of us can do, is to continue to try. That is all I ask of myself. It is all you should ask of yourself.

# 17

# The Fear of Loss of Control: The Hidden Obstacle to Forgiveness

**I**f forgiving makes such sense, why is it so hard to do? Forgiving is difficult for the same reasons that falling upwards is difficult. Our human nature heads in the other direction. We are drawn to keeping distance and holding grudges with the same certain pull that our feet are clamped to the ground. Our strongest instincts lead us to blame, not to forgive.

Resentful feelings grab us, while forgiving ones patiently wait, hoping to be noticed. Hatred—or its subdued cousins, anger and resentment—grab you and won't let you go, while forgiveness slips past you like a shadow. The more severe the hurt that has been done you, the more difficult it is to free yourself from the hatred that entwines you automatically, like some flesh-eating vine, from the moment you get hurt, while forgiveness hardly even enters your mind.

Stopping short of revenge feels so incomplete, like singing "Ahh" without adding "men" at the end of a hymn, or saying "Humpty" without adding "Dumpty." It just feels wrong.

We are wired as deeply as our musical sense or sense of

balance to respond to hurt with hurt, pain with pain, insult with insult.

Not doing so requires enormous restraint. It can feel as difficult and unnatural as keeping your eyes open when you sneeze. It is not something we humans are biologically equipped to do. It goes against the deepest grain of our survival instincts.

Not only are we instinctually opposed to forgiving, we are psychologically and emotionally against it as well. Part of what makes hatred so irresistible is that hatred feels so good, like cold water applied to a burn. Once you have been hurt, you naturally soothe yourself by hating the person who hurt you.

Finally, at an intellectual level we oppose forgiveness as well. We think that forgiveness is wrong for various well-constructed reasons: it opens us up to further attack; it makes us look weak; it denies the victim justice; it fails to teach the perpetrator a lesson; it leaves us feeling incomplete, aching for "closure"; it sets a bad precedent.

However, I think the deeper reason we oppose forgiveness is the unexamined belief that by hating enough, or by taking revenge, we can somehow change what happened, or at least right the wrong. At the core of this belief burns a secret human wish: Not only do we want to undo the past or right the wrong, we want to change the conditions of life. The condition of life we most want to change is the inevitability of death. Death insults us. It always wins. It mocks our wish for omnipotence and confounds our desire for control.

We believe—or act as if we believe—that by hating enough, or by taking sufficient revenge, we can somehow take back control. By killing enough people, by hating enough enemies, by wiping out all who have or would hurt us, we can take charge. We can rule. We can be in control.

As I see it, hatred and the need for revenge originate in the humiliation, rage and betrayal we feel at lacking control. The fact of death is the ultimate proof of our lack of control. My friend's throwing the rock at his former boss's window was just one minuscule manifestation of the humiliation, rage and betrayal we all might feel—if we stopped to think about it— at the inevitability of death. Getting born only to die, loving only to lose those we love, living only to leave life—these are reasons to rage, or at least throw a few rocks at the house of whoever made up these cruel rules. Robert Frost put it succinctly:

> *Forgive, O Lord, my little jokes on thee*
> *And I'll forgive Thy great big one on me.*

Because the Lord—or whoever made up the rules—is not available to throw rocks at, we throw rocks at one another instead. We humans are angry, and every little insult we endure puts us in mind of the great big one down the line.

Does this sound far-fetched to you? It's not death we are angry at, you might point out, but the person who hurt us.

That is true enough, at least on the surface. If a kid gets beat up on the playground and seeks revenge the next day, he is not doing so out of anger about death, but a desire to hurt the person who hurt him.

However, if you look at how deeply hatred and the rush to revenge run throughout human history and then look at how destructive these forces turn out to be, then you have to wonder why. What's the deeper reason? Why don't we

humans get it? Why haven't we wised up and learned the lessons that the most thoughtful people throughout the ages
have been trying to teach us? Why haven't we learned that
forgiving is in our best interests?

I suggest the deeper reason, the reason that compels us to
ignore all the sages and go furiously on in search of revenge,
is the overpowering fear and vulnerability we feel at the fact
of death. We hate that we lack control, and so we take what
control we can by trying to take revenge. Revenge preserves
the illusion that we are in control, an illusion that death
destroys as fast as we can re-create it. Someone kills my
friend. So I go kill him, as if by killing my friend's killer I could
cancel out the loss I suffered and take back control over the
conditions of my life. Then my friend's killer's friend, driven
by the same motives that drove me, hunts me down and kills
me. On and on it goes. Where it will stop, nobody knows.

We fight and kill as if, by doing so, we go death one
better. We take control away from death—or so we make
believe. It's paradoxical, isn't it? We fight and kill in order
to make believe that death will die, that killing will end, that
we will not be killed. You can then substitute the word
"hurt" for "kill" to take into account the more common
examples when life is not at stake, as for the child on the
playground. Even the child on the playground is fighting in
order to reduce the feeling of vulnerability and augment the
feeling of control and strength. In most of our battles we are
trying to assuage our vulnerability by trying to demonstrate
our strength—instead of joining hands and acknowledging
that we are all utterly vulnerable.

Don't get me wrong. I am not recommending a passive

world of hand-holding and hand-wringing. But I am trying to ferret out the deeper reason for all the carnage we humans have committed, the deeper reason that wars rage on, or, at a more ordinary level, the deeper reason mature adults self-destruct, ripping away at each other after a divorce or destroying a lifelong friendship over a simple slight.

Whenever someone hurts us, we feel an instant desire to hit back—to get even—rather than to return the hurt with forgiveness and love. Hitting back feels better. Hitting back feels powerful. Hitting back allows us to forget that the final loss is *always, always our own.* We all will die. Every act of vengeance, every act of retribution is, at its core, an angry attempt to correct this injustice, the injustice of life created by death. We want to *get even,* to undo the imbalance, to change the rotten rules of this game called life.

But it can't be done, at least not by human hands, at least not on this Earth. Each of us is going to die. We have no recourse. But by taking revenge, by getting even, by focusing on how we can get back at those who have hurt us, we can create the illusion of recourse, as if each act of retribution somehow settles the scales and makes us stronger. But the scales set by death remain tilted against us, and they always, always will. Our real strength lies in accepting this fact and acting accordingly.

Forgiveness recognizes and accepts the imbalance. Forgiveness rises above getting even. Forgiveness looks at life from the grand perspective of Mount Death, and says, "Enough. I will not add to the suffering. Instead, I will forgive."

My friend picked up a stone in the middle of the night and

threw it at the house of the man who had hurt him. We all have done something like that in our lives. Even if my friend, or one of us, had hit the house, what would he have gained? Even if the rock had struck the man as he was leaning out his window and killed him dead on the spot, what would my friend have gained? Even if he had gotten away with murder, even if he had committed the perfect crime with his little stone, what would he have gained?

Satisfaction, you may say. How good it feels to hurt the person who has hurt you. Imagine killing him in the middle of the night and getting away with it. That would teach him a lesson. That would teach him not to humiliate other people; that would teach him what happens when you push someone too far.

But we're all pushed too far. We are asked to live, knowing that we will lose life and those we love. No amount of hatred or revenge can change this.

We humans have one recourse that does change the game. It is not the recourse of throwing stones at the windows of those who hurt us—of taking revenge, of living in hatred—but rather the radical, paradoxical response of forgiveness.

Forgiving means more than waiting until you have forgotten the wrong that was done. Time does that on its own accord, and it requires no effort. Sooner or later, most people forget. Just as sooner or later the splinter will work its way out of your thumb on its own, or find a comfortable resting place in a fleshy pad, so too will most wounds fade into forgetfulness, that realm that numbs all pain.

But active forgiveness is not about numbing. Active forgiveness is about looking at pain and loss and injustice straight on and feeling the hurt through and through and still saying, "I will not return pain with pain. I will extinguish the pain by letting go of my part in it."

When you forgive, you are forgiving not only the person who hurt you, but you are forgiving the conditions of life itself. You are freeing yourself from the chains of rage and resentment at injustice, evil, suffering and death that shackle us all. We forge these chains of rage and resentment, link by link, out of each injustice done to us and to others, the mother lode of injustice being death.

We can choose from many other kinds of injustice as well. The older we get, the more we find. The pain of life weighs us down. It is good to lighten our load, if we can. Forgiveness is one way to lighten the load.

But it remains so difficult to forgive. Even when no one is to blame for the hurt we suffer, it is difficult to forgive.

My double first cousin, Josselyn, who was really like a sister to me, died in 2002 at the age of fifty-six. I felt lost in my life without her when she died, and I still do, all this time later. If I could have blamed someone for her dying, it would have lessened my pain, because then I could have turned my sadness into anger and my anger into a campaign for vengeance, which, when gained, would have felt like a victory, a win, to offset the defeat we who loved her suffered when she died. Instead, I am left with loss.

On the day before she died, she asked me to make her better. I went down to the chapel in the hospital and said a prayer, asking for a miracle. I can still feel the ricketiness of the wooden bench that served as a pew in the tiny hospital chapel, and I can still see the altar made of a table, what

looked like a white cloth napkin, and a brass cross. I looked
at the cross, then I bowed my head. I prayed quickly, as there
seemed to be no time to lose, and I prayed hard, meaning I
closed my eyes tight and squeezed my hands together like
a vise.

I prayed, while my wife, Sue, went to the ladies room and
life everywhere else in the hospital and around the world continued on, unaware of the desperate prayer being said in this
little room in Rhode Island Hospital in Providence, Rhode
Island.

Josselyn died the next day.

At first I blamed myself for not praying hard enough, and
then I blamed God for not doing what I'd asked in my prayer,
and then I didn't know who or what to blame, and my blaming petered out.

Once the blaming passed, I was left with my life, a life
without Josselyn. Her absence lay within me like a cold stone.

It would have been easier to use blame to ease the pain of
the loss. Blame feels good. Blame gives reasons where reasons may not exist. Blame rouses your energy and gives you
a purpose in what you do. Blame is exciting.

But when you forgive, there is no excitement. You are left
with loss and pain, with no blame or anger to support you
through the hard time.

When Josselyn died, I was stunned. So were all of us who
loved her. After she died, it was as if, whenever we went to
sit down, our chairs were always pulled out just as we were
about to sit, and we kept falling onto the floor. So we went,
day after day, falling down over and over again, trying to find
new supports or new ways of sitting and living, but falling

and hurting, time and again, like newly paralyzed people try-ing to learn how to get around in the world.

It would have been great to have someone to blame. *Who keeps pulling out those chairs? Wait until I get my hands on you. And who permanently pulled out Josselyn's chair? Just wait until I get my hands on you!*

But we knew that anger was futile, as futile as complain-ing about the weather. We had to get used to life without her. We are still trying to do that. But life will never be the same. It never is. Each loss changes life forever; the greater the loss, the greater the change.

I see her in my mind all the time: her friendly, tanned face with crinkles around her smiling, wise eyes; the dimples she'd had ever since she was a little girl; and the blonde hair cut short, giving her a peppy, ready-to-go look, even at age fifty-six.

None of us was ready for her to go. She organized the whole extended family. She and her husband, Tom, had five children. The youngest was about to graduate from college when Josselyn died, and the oldest was a resident in emer-gency room medicine in the hospital where she did die. No one was ready for any of it.

A friend told me that forgiveness is so hard because it rep-resents giving up on the wish that the past will be different. I learned how true that was when Josselyn died. Maybe the greatest obstacle to forgiveness is hope. As long as you are hoping that the past will change, you can be angry that it hasn't.

When I forgave whatever the force is that took
I call it God—I gave up my hope that she hadn't d

up on my wish that the past would change, that come tomorrow, she would walk back into our lives and tell us it was all a joke, that she'd just wanted to see how we'd all react. But it wasn't a joke. The past was not going to change.

I think that's one reason that people file lawsuits. Not only for the money, but to keep alive the hope that the past will be different, that the bad thing that happened did not happen. But I couldn't file suit against life or God.

To sue and fight and pitch a fit is much easier than to accept what happens in life.

At the core, that's what makes forgiving so difficult. It is the same as what makes living difficult: the inevitability of loss. It is difficult to live with clocks and to notice what the passage of time really means. It is difficult to forgive yesterday for becoming today and today for its unrelenting insistence on becoming tomorrow. It is difficult to give up hope that the past will be different and that the future won't take what we love. But it will, and it does.

Before she died Josselyn was fighting cancer as hard as anyone could fight. But she also used to say, "What will be, will be." I used to get angry with her for saying that, and say, "No, we can do better than that." She would smile. She was smiling at my naiveté, at my hope, I guess, and at her love for me, for all of us, for life. That made her smile. At the very end, it made her cry. She didn't want to leave any more than we wanted her to go.

She always used to say that she wanted to be sure she didn't die until her children didn't need her anymore, at least until they had all graduated from college. She almost made it hat far. She only missed by a couple of months. But I can tell

you her children wouldn't say that they don't need her anymore, anymore than I would say that I don't need her now,
and I am fifty-two. We humans never stop needing each
other.

The oldest child, her daughter, Molly, the ER doctor, lay
next to her in bed rubbing her back the day before she died,
telling her stories of all the great family vacations they had
taken. And they had taken many. To Disney World, to Cape
Cod where Josselyn had grown up, to ranches and fishing
country out west, to a villa in Jamaica, and many, many
more. Molly told her about those as she rubbed her back.
Josselyn would squeeze her hand now and then, as if to say,
"I hear you. I love you."

They both knew the moments of life were winding down.
Molly was trying to make her mother's last few hours on
Earth as good as she could, and her mother was trying to stay
just as long as life would let her.

But then, after one last, deep breath, she didn't breathe
again. She was gone.

We all gathered to say good-bye in various ways. There
was a Quaker memorial service, as Josselyn was a Quaker
when she acknowledged any religion. We didn't fight with
each other as families so often do when someone dies. We
seemed to forgive each other for the little annoying things we
each did, as we swam around in the sea of sadness that surrounded this death. We all had an idea how each other was
feeling, and we wanted to help each other out, even though
none of us could do what we each really wanted to do,
namely to bring her back.

This incapacity, too, is at the heart of forgiveness. You

can't do what you really want to do. You can't make the bad thing that happened never have happened. But you can do, or at least try to do, the next best thing, which is forgive what has happened. You can try to make the hurt end right there. You can let the anger rise up within you like a fire, then burn itself out, rather than let it set another fire. This is the good that comes out of forgiveness. Nobody else gets hurt. You take the burn, then you heal. You don't spread the fire.

Josselyn was right. What will be, will be. And what was, was. She has died. It does me no good to rage against God or fate or life or myself or her doctors and nurses or cancer or the human condition or the politicians who didn't provide money for research or anything else that I might think of raging against—and I have thought of all of those.

I can put some effort into making sure deaths like hers don't happen as often, say, by trying to raise money for research. Forgiving does not mean becoming passive; nor does it mean ceasing to take steps to prevent the bad thing from happening again, including subjecting the offender, if there is one, to a suitable consequence. Forgiveness does not mean passing laws to prevent the bad things from happening again.

But forgiveness does mean that you cease to let yourself be consumed with anger, resentment, bitterness and the other volatile solvents that keep the fire burning, a fire that spreads, destroying families, towns, even countries.

Forgiveness proceeds person by person. When Josselyn died, I had to let my anger rise, burn and subside. Now it is just a set of glowing coals. In place of the flames, a warming love is settling in—my love for her, her love for us—and I feel it every day. The awful chill of her absence remains, but the warmth of her love lives on as well.

To get on with life in a good way, I had to give up my hope that the past will be different. I had to forgive life for being what it is.

But it is so difficult to forgive, just as it can be so difficult to live.

If we can accept that we lack control, if we look at death and accept it without rage, then the chains that keep us unforgiving and angry can begin to break and disappear. We can then rise above what holds us down, namely anger, resentment and hatred. We become free.

# 18

# The Greatest Challenge

I happen to be a Christian, an Episcopalian to be exact. But I am writing this book from the standpoint of a secular human being, filled with doubts and questions, not the standpoint of a Christian or a believer of any kind.

I am perplexed by the challenge forgiveness poses, as well as inspired by the outrageous, dazzling chance it dares us to take. If we all could ever figure out how to do what Jesus asked people to—namely to love their neighbors, even their enemies—then this world would find peace, whether or not anybody believed in God, Jesus, Santa Claus or any spirit whatsoever. I refer to the words of Jesus of Nazareth only because they are some of the most helpful—as well as challenging—ever written about forgiveness.

The great challenge—which I think is the greatest challenge ever put to us humans—is put succinctly in the Gospel of Luke. Jesus says:

> Love your enemies, do good to those who hate you, bless those who curse you, pray for those who abuse

you. If anyone strikes you on the cheek, offer the other also; and from anyone who takes away your coat do not withhold even your shirt. Give to everyone who begs from you; and if anyone takes away your goods, do not ask for them again. Do to others as you would have them do to you. (Luke 6:27–31)

Have you ever met anyone who actually *does* all that? I haven't. I'm sure there are some, but I don't know any. I suppose the Dalai Lama does. And a few other very unusual people. But I haven't met one.

In fact, I have met very few who even try. People who do that are uncommon souls. Our laws and morality are so rooted in the principle of getting even—one wrong should beget an equal and opposite wrong—that Jesus' words seem all but insane. "Dream on, Jesus," we say. "Get real."

I mean, *really,* can you imagine walking down a street in any American city and giving your money or your jacket or your shirt to each person who begs from you? You'd be flat broke by the time you'd gone two blocks. You'd also be naked, and you'd probably be dead.

Jesus' advice, which appears in other forms in most religions, is so impractical that we laugh at it or simply ignore it in secular life. It is revered only by an anomalous few. Nobody I know raises their children to turn the other cheek or to give their personal possessions to everyone who begs from them. Nobody I know would refrain from asking that their goods be returned, if they were stolen. Jesus' plan is just plain ridiculous! What kind of world did he think we were living in? Even the most devout and ardent Christians don't follow Jesus' advice.

If practically no one, not even rock-solid Christians, follows Jesus' plan, then what good is it? Isn't it an irrelevant curiosity, like the fortune in a Chinese cookie? How can I maintain that it is so helpful, if all it does is make us laugh at what an impractical dreamer Jesus was or feel glum that none of us can be anything like him?

I say Jesus' words are helpful because they can get us started doing what needs to be done. They can start us questioning our usually unquestioned desire for revenge.

Revenge may even be just, but is justice always right? Are there times when we should put an end to an evil cycle by accepting injustice and not fighting back? Knowing we humans will never do this, Jesus still challenges us to try.

He elaborates the challenge in the next verse:

> If you love those who love you, what credit is that to you? For even sinners love those who love them. If you do good to those who do good to you, what credit is that to you? For even sinners do the same. If you lend to those from whom you hope to receive, what credit is that to you? Even sinners lend to sinners, to receive as much again. But love your enemies, do good, and lend, expecting nothing in return. Your reward will be great. (Luke 6:32–35a)

In what is perhaps the most impractical, unfollowable advice ever given, Jesus asks us to confound our human nature and love our enemies. It seems as impossible as asking that two plus two suddenly equal five.

But if you try, you will find that even if you don't end up loving your enemies, you will have put the brakes on the rampaging virus of rage that can sweep through individuals, families, towns and countries.

You try to love your enemies not by willing yourself to do so out of obligation—that's called faking it—but by using your imagination to develop empathy. Try to understand how your enemy, a fellow human being, became so evil, at least in your eyes. Try to be a lawyer making a case for your enemy in court, or try to be a writer thinking of some way to make this rotten character be balanced and believable, instead of two-dimensionally, purely evil. As you use your imagination, as you grit your teeth and try to understand this person whom you detest, you will find if not love, at least something like love taking hold of your heart.

Not only is this good for you, the future of this world depends upon people learning how to do it.

Jesus is not alone in asking this. Every great teacher, from Moses to Muhammad to Buddha to Confucius, has asked us to oppose our natural tendencies in one way or another. To do what is right, we often need *not* to do what we naturally want to do. Never is this truer than when we seek revenge.

Jesus then goes on to speak paradoxically, as those who reach the heart of human experience so often do. He says:

> Do not judge, and you will not be judged; do not condemn, and you will not be condemned. Forgive, and you will be forgiven; give, and it will be given to you. (Luke 6:37–38a)

There we see the strange contradiction Jesus offers as the solution to the problem of evil. If we will forgive, then we will be forgiven. Forgive us our trespasses, as we forgive those who trespass against us. Give and you will receive. Or, as in the prayer of St. Francis, "It is in pardoning that we are pardoned. It is in dying to the self that we are born to eternal life."

*What?* This is all just too paradoxical, too counterintuitive. It is absurd. It doesn't make any sense at all. Not only do these teachings of Jesus seem to make no sense, but also the teachings of Buddha, of Muhammad, of all the people who claim to have seen beyond where most of us can see. Even the Old Testament, famous for its depiction of an angry, vengeful, "just" God, says in Leviticus: "You shall not take vengeance or bear a grudge against any of your people, but you shall love your neighbor as yourself." Each of your neighbors, not just the ones you like.

What is in it for a person to do *that?* Wouldn't it just turn us into victims of the wolves who surround us?

And even if we wanted to forgive our enemies—a few of us actually do want to do that—how on Earth could we? It so goes against our grain. It is like telling us not to feel envy, anger, jealousy, sexual attraction or fear. It is like telling us not to feel thirst, or instructing us to fall upwards. It is like telling us not to be human. It is also like telling us to jettison reason. Revenge is reasonable; it makes sense. Forgiveness, on the other hand, is unreasonable. It seems preposterous. How then do we bring ourselves to do the preposterous, to do what feels utterly contrary to what we are in every way inclined by nature to do?

We bring ourselves to do it by knowing that it is what's best. We bring ourselves to do it by talking the pain out, over and over again, until the anger and resentment finally wash away. Weary with the work of getting there, we can finally repose upon the stability of forgiveness, a clear, uncluttered place where we can see how good it is that we got there.

We bring ourselves to do it in our own private ways. I have given a method in this book, and I have offered examples of various people who managed to forgive. How you do it, if you do it, is up to you. If you are able to go reason one better and forgive, you will have lifted yourself to a better place. Of that I am sure.

Let me close this chapter with one of the most "unreasonable" examples of forgiveness I have ever found.

Some years ago, a seven-year-old girl named Susie was kidnapped from her tent on a camping trip and later murdered. Her mother, Marietta Jaeger, at first knew only that Susie had been kidnapped. She wrote:

> While I prepared for bed that night, very consciously and deliberately and with much premeditation, I said out loud to my husband, "Even if the kidnapper were to bring Susie back, alive and well, this very moment, I could still kill him for what he has done to my family." I believed I could have done so with my bare hands and a big smile on my face, if only I knew who he was. Almost as soon as the words were uttered, however human a response as their sentiment was, I knew that to give myself to that ugly mind-set would violate the principles and value system I held. Also, I'd learned enough about psychological well-being to know that hatred was not healthy. . . . Still, I was utterly furious. I felt absolutely justified in my

desire for revenge. . . . I knew the death penalty could be an option, and I was unabashedly convinced that this person should get "the chair." Susie was an innocent, defenseless little girl; I had every right to avenge whatever had happened to her. And so, round and round I went, wrestling with the worst and the best of myself.

Finally, because I'd been well taught always to reach for the highest moral ground, I surrendered. I made a decision to forgive this person, whoever he was. Yet, so saying I clearly understood that this was not an accomplished feat by any means. The best I could muster was to begin to choose to make a serious effort to measure up to the call of my conscience. My choice seemed to lift an enormous burden from my heart, and for the first time since Susie had been taken, I actually was able to sleep soundly and felt rested in the morning.

Marietta still didn't know what had happened to Susie. But she had decided to forgive the person who had taken her. Usually, when forgiveness is difficult, it gets started with a conscious decision like this to try. The decision often originates, as it did with Marietta, in some system of values, a philosophy or a religion. Oddly enough, vengeance can be rooted in the very same place. We can believe in forgiveness, or we can believe in vengeance, and back up either belief with scripture, law or even the codes of Hammurabi if we want to. It is not enough to be a Christian or a Muslim or a Jew to know if you will decide to forgive; it is not even enough to be one who believes in the rule of law to know if you will advocate mercy.

You have to be at a certain place in your development as a human being. You may not subscribe to any religion at all, you may not believe in any kind of god, and you may not give a hoot about the law. The decision to try to forgive reflects more the kind of person you are than the beliefs you think you adhere to. Sometimes you surprise yourself when you decide to try to forgive.

Deciding to forgive was only the beginning for Marietta, as it is for anyone who wants to forgive a grievous wrong. The braking system of her beliefs slowed her down from the rush to vengeance, but reaching forgiveness takes a lot more than the desire to forgive. Forgiveness, especially for something as horrible as what Marietta was trying to forgive, is beyond difficult. It can feel impossible, requiring a miracle. As Marietta wrote:

> I've heard people say that forgiveness is for wimps. Well, I say then that they must never have tried it. Forgiveness is hard work. It demands diligent self-discipline, constant corralling of our basest instincts, custody of the tongue, and a steadfast refusal not to get caught up in the mean-spiritedness of our times. It doesn't mean we forget, we condone, or we absolve responsibility. It does mean that we let go of hate, that we try to separate the loss and the cost from the recompense or punishment we deem is due.

As Marietta was working on forgiving her daughter's abductor, she still didn't know where her daughter was. A year passed after the kidnapping, with no sign of Susie.

Marietta was then quoted in the newspaper that she felt concern not only for her daughter but for the kidnapper as well, and that she wished she could speak to him herself. The kidnapper must have read what Marietta said.

The night the report appeared, in the middle of the night—one year to the very minute he had taken Susie out of our tent—this man telephoned me at our home in Michigan.

He woke me from a sound sleep, but I knew who he was immediately. It quickly became clear he was calling to taunt me: "You wanted to talk to me? Well, here I am! Now what are you going to do about it? Because no one is ever going to find out who I am, and I am the one who is calling the shots. So what does it matter if you get to talk to me or not?"

To my amazement, as smug and nasty as he was being, something utterly unforeseen began to happen in me. From that time a year before, in Montana, where I had surrendered my rage and desire for revenge, I had truly tried to cooperate with moving my heart from fury to forgiveness.

She then recounts the tenets of her Christian belief that she had been reminding herself of ever since she had "surrendered" her rage and desire for revenge, and tried to "cooperate with moving my heart from fury to forgiveness." She reminded herself that the kidnapper was a child of God, just as her daughter was. How could she do that at that moment? How could she feel anything but hatred for this man who had taken her daughter and was now taunting her on the telephone?

She could do it because the process of forgiveness had started in her long, long ago. Probably her genetic makeup even helped. Forgiveness usually comes more naturally for women than for men. Beyond genes that made her a woman, there were probably other genes, genes that govern temperament and mood, that made her the kind of person who could forgive even the greatest of hurts.

But genes were far from enough. She had practiced forgiveness since she was a child. She subscribed to a system of belief that put forgiveness above vengeance. That system was stitched into her nervous system, so when the moment of truth arrived, the desire to forgive rose up almost as reflexively as the rage and desire for revenge.

But even that was not enough. She had to work, "surrendering" her rage and desire for revenge, and "cooperating" within herself to move her heart from fury to forgiveness.

Her lifetime of preparation, especially her work since the kidnapping, culminated in that middle-of-the-night telephone call, when "something utterly unforeseen began to happen in me." She was able to "separate the loss and the cost from the recompense or punishment" she deemed was due. She wrote:

> This is what happened to me, all that I had been working for, as I heard, for the first time, this man's voice in my ear—and neither of us was expecting it.
>
> He was taken aback, backed off from his taunts, gentled down, and stayed on the phone for over an hour, even though he repeatedly expressed fear that the call

was being traced and that he'd be caught speaking to me. When I asked him what I could to help him, he lost control and wept. Finally, he said, "I wish this burden could be lifted from me." I certainly knew the possibilities of what "this burden" could be, but I couldn't get him to elaborate. However, that's when I really understood the transformation that had happened to me. As desperate as I was for Susie's return, I also realized I wanted to reach and help this man.

Marietta does not say she felt the man did not deserve punishment, only that she was able to "separate the loss and the cost from the recompense or punishment" and return to being the person she had always asked herself to be: someone who reaches out and tries to understand others, loving them as herself, no matter who they might be or what they might have done.

It turned out that the man on the phone in fact had murdered Susie. Marietta spoke at his sentencing.

Though he was liable for the death penalty, I felt it would violate and profane the goodness, sweetness, and beauty of Susie's life by killing the kidnapper in her name. She was deserving of a more noble and beautiful memorial than a cold-blooded, premeditated, state-sanctioned killing of a restrained, defenseless man, however deserving of death he may be deemed to be. I felt I far better honored her, not by becoming that which I deplored, but by saying that all life is sacred and worthy of preservation.

Marietta's request was honored. The man's life was spared and he was sent to prison.

Who gained from all of this? A child killer had his life spared. He gained, I suppose, although you have to wonder what life was like for him in prison.

Who else gained? Susie was gone. Her family and friends had a lifetime of missing her to look forward to. Wouldn't they feel better off during those years if they knew Susie's killer was not being cared for and kept alive? Wouldn't they feel better if the killer was dead?

Let me let Marietta answer that question:

Though I readily admit that initially I wanted to kill this man with my bare hands, by the time of the resolution of his crimes, I was convinced that my best and healthiest option was to forgive. In the twenty years since losing my daughter, I have been working with victims and their families, and my experience has been consistently confirmed. Victim families have every right initially to the normal, valid, human response of rage, but those persons who retain a vindictive mind-set ultimately give the offender another victim. Embittered, tormented, enslaved by the past, their quality of life is diminished. However justified, our unforgiveness undoes us. Anger, hatred, resentment, bitterness, revenge—they are death-dealing spirits, and they will "take our lives" on some level as surely as Susie's life was taken. I believe the only way we can be whole, healthy, happy persons is to learn to forgive. This is the inexorable lesson and experience of the gospel of

Marietta. Though I would never have chosen it so, the first person to receive a gift of life from the death of my daughter . . . was me.

# Conclusion
# Now That We Must, Can We?
# A Global Perspective

So far, I have stressed how forgiveness improves our individual lives. I have left to the end the obvious extension of that idea: the need for and the benefits of forgiveness worldwide. The dream of peace is a dream almost every one of us entertains, even little children in school. In one school I visited recently, the most common dream among fourth-graders was global peace. I am sure that is the case in many thousands of other schools around the world. Children know we need to learn how to forgive. How about us?

Vengeance is a luxury this world can no longer afford, if it ever could. Now that we have nuclear weapons and other tools that can decimate our world, we are left to struggle every day to make sure someone doesn't actually use them.

For some time now, human life on Earth has been able to wipe itself out. We have grown so accustomed to this horrible possibility that it hardly disturbs us or even feels horrible. It's old news. For decades, we have been set up to destroy ourselves every single night and every single day. Like dogs of hell, our weapons never sleep. They obediently wait for one short command. What has stifled that command so far is the discipline of a small collection of individual human beings. All our lives, and all future life on Earth, depends now upon the wisdom and restraint of these very few people. How much faith do you have in them?

One of them could decide to give the order today or tomorrow. Honestly, it amazes me someone didn't give it yesterday, or the many other yesterdays this world has survived. As the years pass, we have loaded more and more weapons, turning our world into a poised-and-ready suicide bomber. Somehow or other, miracle of miracles, this globe-bomber hasn't run its mission yet. But how long will our luck last?

Even though we don't like to think about such stuff, we must know that before we see our children grow up, or before we meet our grandchildren, we may have obliterated ourselves. Can't happen, you say? If Pearl Harbor and Hiroshima didn't teach us, September 11 taught us that what can't happen can and does happen.

Each day that passes without our having cooked our planet should make us all stop and say "Whew!"—and then make plans to change the way we act in this world. We should stop taking our continued existence for granted and realize that we are surviving in spite of ourselves.

Thousands if not tens of thousands of people in the world today are so fanatical and full of hatred that they would relish the chance to set off the bombs or release the poisons that would lead to the end of life. That we have had the tools to do so and have not done it for this long is, well, improbable. Can't we develop a better strategy than luck before our luck runs out?

One solution is to take away the tools that make mass annihilation possible.

Another is to change human nature.

You probably have to do the second to achieve the first. So neither will happen.

But there is a third way. We can't change human nature, but we can push it beyond its current limits. We can progress. New strategies could grow out of a worldwide effort, a gradual rising up of ordinary people in villages and cities and jungles and deserts all over the world, everyday people who are not the types who usually join causes or band together but who recognize the need to do something definite before it's too late.

If the sun disappeared, what would happen? People would recognize the emergency and we'd all band together to do something about it. Of course, in that case, we'd have no time. We'd be dead before we'd had a chance to think out a solution. But now, we do have time. The sun has not yet disappeared. Whatever force rules this universe has given us time to figure out a better way. But the time will not last forever. Ordinary people, not fanatics, must save us.

We all know that we have killed too many of each other. I feel within myself, and I sense within others around the world, a voice that cries, "Enough! We are tired of seeing children get killed by bullets or bombs or starvation or preventable diseases. We are tired of the stinking mess we are making out of this blessed planet. And we are tired of not doing anything about it." The anguish that many people feel is gradually finding its voice in previously silent mouths everywhere.

Is it naive to believe we can make a lasting peace? Is it impossible? Naive, of course. But no, it's not impossible, no more impossible than any other miracle.

So what can we do? It is one thing if you are president or king or queen, or prime minister or dictator or chief or premier; then you can give orders and make policies. But what if you are just you or me? What can we do? I ask myself that question sometimes, and I shrug, as if to say it's beyond me, it's not my job, what will be will be, and the best I can do is to be as good a person as I'm up to being, which I have enough trouble with on its own.

I have bills to pay, the dentist to go to, projects to work on and worries to worry over, and all those are quite enough to keep me more than busy day after day. I don't have time to join a cause, and even if I did, I don't know what cause I would join.

The cause to save the world? Causes like that are for fools. What good are all of these noble causes doing anyway? We're still on the brink of disaster. *Nothing works,* I say to myself. *What happens happens. Let's make the best of what we've got while we can. End of discussion.*

But then I think of my cousin, Josselyn, who died at the age of fifty-six. She was a fixer. She fixed people's lives. If I ever said to her, "Causes fail," or "Nothing will work," she would have said, "Well, get off your lazy butt and do something to try to help anyway."

So, I'm writing this book. In the great scheme, that's not much, but it's something. And you're reading this book. That's not much either, but it's something. We're trying. That leads to progress.

We all have a skill or two. If we each tap into our skills and offer what we can, we can generate enough of that invisible, immeasurable force called goodness to contain and subdue the invisible, immeasurable force called evil.

What have I to offer? What can I do to promote the flow of positive energy in my corner of the world? What more can I do? I can be good to my kids, pat my dogs, be kind to the person who delivers my mail and, as I said before, try to be as decent a person as I'm able to be. That's a lot. But what more? The world needs more. A whole lot more. Is there a next step, a more potent way?

Yes, there is. Forgive. Learn to stop being ruled by anger and the desire for revenge. Work toward forgiving those we feel we can't forgive: the murderers, the rapists, the psychopaths and the fanatics.

In the United States, we could each begin by trying to understand well enough to forgive what happened on September 11, 2001. Remember, by "forgive" I mean disown the anger and resentment, cease to live under its rule. The anger and resentment will kill us all, unless we get out from under. As much as we deplore what happened on September 11, as much as we hate that it happened and saw our country ravaged by it and friends ruined by it, we could, if we would, try to do what is really the only action we can take to undo the evil: Forgive it. Put down our vengeance. Rise beyond hate rather than seek to return it in kind.

Melissa Turnage from Cockeysville, Maryland, lost her son, Adam, on September 11. He was an environmentalist, working at Cantor Fitzgerald in one of the Twin Towers. The terrorists killed Adam.

Melissa has forgiven those terrorists. "I didn't go through any specific steps to forgive them," she told me. "The first time I was asked the question, I think I forgave them right then. I felt sadness, tremendous sadness, over the fact that anyone would feel comfortable killing thousands of people."

But how did she do it? How did she find it within her to extinguish the rage she must have felt at what the terrorists did? "I honestly feel that those men were wounded children. Maybe because I am a schoolteacher and I see the effects that adults can have on children, I see those terrorists as wounded children." She went on to say, "Look, violence begets violence. Until we figure that out, the world won't change. We will keep doing it over and over again."

Melissa's solution was this: "I think we've got to empower the women more. They are the ones who can teach empathy and compassion. They can start to teach now because lots of people are desperate for answers. So, they are ready to learn.

"What happened on September 11 was so big that if we could take it and turn it into a movement of forgiveness here, look at the power we'd have globally. We could start to change the world. We hold that possibility in our hands now."

How do we ordinary people join forces with heroes like Melissa Turnage or Marietta Jaeger? By hearing their message, agreeing with it and trying to do likewise in the smaller ways life offers us every day—until one of the big ways comes along, which it most certainly will.

Just think of Marietta Jaeger, who forgave the man who killed her daughter and spoke against his receiving the death penalty. Or think of Melissa Turnage, who forgave the "wounded child" who murdered her child. If they could do that, we too should be able to forgive. Forgiving the killers does not equal approval. It only means that we refuse to be governed by the wish for revenge.

In this world-weary world, where cynics hold sway, you might object that for every Marietta Jaeger or Melissa Turnage, a million others demand revenge. You might add that it is painfully obvious that while certain individuals may make peace, humanity has proven beyond all doubt that it never will.

To the cynic I say, "Get off your lazy butt and do something about it anyway." Or, as the more articulate and dour William the Silent said centuries ago, "It is not necessary to hope in order to undertake, nor to prevail in order to persevere." If we die, we at least should die trying to stop death, not perpetuating it. We should not measure the worth of the task by its probable outcome.

If we dare to try, we can generate such a wave of positive energy as the world has never seen, enough to move human nature out of its deadlocked place into a new set of habits and trends. Such an energy will electrify the air and set off bolts of dry lightning, causing cynics everywhere to rediscover what they'd given up on. We each can do this, each in our own ways.

You don't believe it? Children do it every day.

All we adults have to do is give it a shot.

The greatest challenge we humans now face is not scientific or technological or even economic. It is emotional. It is playground basic, playground simple and playground tough. It is how to make peace and forgive people who hurt us.

In your own life, you know where you could begin. You

know who you need to forgive. In this country, we know who our targets have been, from African Americans to Jews to Catholics to fat people to short people to crazy people to Republicans to Democrats to rich people to people on welfare to, well, anyone who is not exactly like us. Even the people like us don't escape our judgment and wrath.

Our latest demon, for obvious reasons, is Muslims.

But the real demon is in you and in me. The real demon is the ignorance and fear that lead to the hatred that leads to the judgments that lead to the killings and wars.

No one is free of it. All we can do is try to refuse to live under its rule. All we can do is try to forgive.

If we don't consolidate our best energies—our hopes and prayers and thoughts and actions—into something more powerful than revenge, then one day that began like any other will end as no day ever has. We will finally use the awful tools we've made, and we will be no more.

How do we avoid that? How can we learn to forgive? How can we put an end to killing each other? From injured nations to injured races to injured individuals, the urge to take revenge has dominated all of human history. For thousands of years, people have been losing their lives in the name of vengeance, retribution and the righting of wrongs, all of which were supposed to end with justice. And still the world is not just. To remedy that, we propose to kill some more.

How can anyone stop such a juggernaut? No one person can. Jesus couldn't. Muhammad couldn't. Nor could any of the prophets who have ever lived.

We must learn the art of forgiveness. We must learn how to respect those we don't understand, those we fear and even hate, whether they be Muslims or Christians or the man who lives down the block. We must disown our hate, learn from those we fear and forgive the murderers.

We will do it. We will do it the same way we have done everything else we absolutely had to do. A force inside us we don't understand will invite us to act, and we will act, and we will grow beyond who we've been, and we will change the way we live.

Will we do it in time?

I believe we will—because we must.

# Appendix:

## Other Approaches to Forgiveness

The approach to forgiveness that I advocate in this book is one based upon imagination—the creative use of empathy—reinforced by conscious effort. The motivation to make such an effort, as I see it, comes from the knowledge that you yourself are better off if you have forgiven than if you carry anger and resentment with you and the knowledge that the world is better off, too. In other words, when you forgive, everyone benefits; and when you don't, everyone suffers. That should be enough to make us all want to forgive.

But there are many other approaches to forgiveness. I want to summarize several of them here and tell you where you can learn more about each of them.

❋    ❋    ❋

The best source is the vast imaginative world literature on forgiveness. Forgiveness and revenge are central themes in the greatest stories, from the Greek tragedies to Shakespeare, as well as the New Testament, the Old Testament, the Koran, the Book of Mormon and most other religious texts.

In addition, a small but growing body of writing based on empirical research into forgiveness is emerging from psychology, theology, the social sciences and medicine. This body of work looks at the "how-to" and "why-to" of forgiveness.

Among these books, one of my favorites is *Wounds Not Healed by Time: The Power of Repentance and Forgiveness,* by Solomon Schimmel, a professor of Jewish education and psychology at Hebrew College in Newton, Massachusetts. Although Schimmel is an academic, his book is totally engrossing.

He divides the process of forgiveness into four phases, and subdivides each phase into units. Phase one is uncovering. Next is the decision phase, in which you consider forgiveness as an option. Third comes the work phase, in which you accept pain and offer compassion. Fourth is the phase Schimmel calls "deepening."

This fourth phase is what makes his method particularly useful, I think, because he shows how an act of forgiveness can lead to growth and transformation for both the individual and those around him or her. Comparing forgiveness to running a marathon, Schimmel writes, "One benefit of completing the difficult journey of forgiveness is the self-knowledge you will acquire that you can overcome powerful negative emotions and are capable of great self-restraint."

Other experts have developed other good methods. Everett Worthington, one of the leaders in the field of forgiveness—yes, it is actually a field of scientific research now, thank goodness—has developed an excellent five-step approach to forgiveness that he summarizes with the acronym REACH:

**R**ecall the hurt,

**E**mpathize with one who hurt you, offer the

**A**ltruistic gift of forgiveness, make a

**C**ommitment to forgive, and

**H**old onto the forgiveness. (Worthington, *Dimensions of Forgiveness,* 108)

You can find Dr. Worthington's method laid out in detail, as well as essays by other experts, in a book he contributed to and edited, *Dimensions of Forgiveness.*

In another excellent book, *Forgiveness Is a Choice,* Dr. Robert Enright divides the process of forgiving into four phases:

1. Uncover your anger.
2. Decide to forgive.
3. Work on forgiveness.
4. Discover and gain release from emotional prison.

Enright is one of the pioneers in the field; all of his writings are outstanding.

Another outstanding expert, Dr. Fred Luskin, has developed a program at Stanford that he lays out in his book *Forgive for Good.* Luskin's method is summed up in the acronym, HEAL.

**H** stands for hope. The first step is to make a positive statement of what you hoped would happen. The statement must be positive ("I hoped for a strong friendship") as opposed to negative ("I hoped he wouldn't betray me").

**E** stands for educate. You need to educate yourself, or

remind yourself, of the limitations of your own control in the given situation and in life.

**A** stands for affirm. You now make a positive statement affirming some goal that the process of forgiveness will lead to. For example, "I intend to become wiser in friendships."

**L** stands for long-term commitment. You make a long-term commitment to practice the HEAL method and make forgiveness a permanent part of your life.

Another expert, Lewis Smedes, in his book, *The Art of Forgiving,* recommends a three-step process. "We rediscover the humanity of the person who hurt us. We surrender our right to get even. We revise our feeling toward the person we forgive."

Charles Klein, a rabbi, explains in his book *How to Forgive When You Can't Forget* a process that leads to what he calls "Reconciliation Day." As he puts it, "For any one of us, 'Reconciliation Day' can come right now—and joy and gladness can once again be our tomorrow." Klein doesn't have a step-by-step method or an acronym that sums up his approach, but his short book is a gem. He reminds us of the various ways in which we harden our hearts, and he urges us, using biblical examples as well as true examples from modern life, to find the healing perspective and to look for the greater good—before it is too late. As he puts it, "You can forgive even when you can't forget. And only you can answer the age-old question, 'If not now, when?'"

Psychoanalyst Salman Akhtar wrote a paper entitled "Forgiveness: Origins, Dynamics, Psychopathology, and Technical Resistance," published in the *Psychoanalytic Quarterly* (vol. LXXI, 2002). Although the article was intended for a professional audience, it is a superb short essay for the general reader if you don't mind a bit of psychoanalytic jargon.

Akhtar sees forgiveness proceeding in three stages:

Revenge
Reparation
Reconsideration

Akhtar is one of the few experts to acknowledge the importance of revenge, in reality or in fantasy. As he puts it, ". . . some revenge is actually good for the victim. It puts the victim's hitherto passive ego in an active position. This imparts a sense of mastery and enhances self-esteem." He also stresses that forgiveness is a kind of mourning and is therefore psychologically invaluable.

Still other methods exist, developed by other experts. But most of the methods share certain aspects: an acknowledging of anger and pain; a reconstituting of the hurtful event in your imagination in some way; allowing for sad feelings to enter in and developing a realistic means for getting past them; a conscious choice to move toward forgiveness and away from anger; and some kind of long-term practice of holding onto forgiveness day after day, which leads you to grow into a deeper, stronger person.

# Selected Bibliography

Arendt, Hannah. *The Human Condition.* Chicago: University of Chicago Press, 1958.

Casarjian, Robin. *Forgiveness: A Bold Choice for a Peaceful Heart.* New York: Bantam Books, 1992.

Enright, Robert D. *Forgiveness Is a Choice.* Washington, D.C.: APA LifeTools, 2001.

Enright, Robert D., and Joanna North, eds.: *Exploring Forgiveness.* Madison: University of Wisconsin Press, 1998.

Karen, Robert. *The Forgiving Self: The Road from Resentment to Connection.* New York: Doubleday, 2001.

Lieberman, David J. *Make Peace with Anyone.* New York: St. Martin's Press, 2002.

Luskin, Fred. *Forgive for Good.* San Francisco: HarperSan-Francisco, 2002.

Schimmel, Solomon. *Wounds Not Healed by Time.* New York: Oxford University Press, 2002.

Smedes, Lewis B. *The Art of Forgiving.* New York: Ballantine Books, 1996.

Wiesenthal, Simon. *The Sunflower: On the Possibilities and*

*Limits of Forgiveness.* New York: Schocken Books, 1998 (originally published in German; Paris: Opera Mundi, 1969).

Worthington, Everett L., ed. *Dimensions of Forgiveness: Psychological Research and Theological Perspectives.* Radnor, Pa.: Templeton Foundation Press, 1998.